Be Domes Dæge

EARLY ENGLISH TEXT SOCIETY

Original Series, No. 65

1876 (reprinted 1964)

PRICE 30s.

Be Domes Dæge,

De Die Judicii,

AN OLD ENGLISH VERSION OF THE LATIN POEM
ASCRIBED TO BEDE.

EDITED (WITH OTHER SHORT POEMS) FROM THE UNIQUE MS. IN THE
LIBRARY OF CORPUS CHRISTI COLLEGE, CAMBRIDGE,

BY

J. RAWSON LUMBY

Published for
THE EARLY ENGLISH TEXT SOCIETY
by the
OXFORD UNIVERSITY PRESS
LONDON   NEW YORK   TORONTO

OXFORD
UNIVERSITY PRESS

Great Clarendon Street, Oxford OX2 6DP
United Kingdom

Oxford University Press is a department of the University of Oxford.
It furthers the University's objective of excellence in research, scholarship,
and education by publishing worldwide. Oxford is a registered trade mark of
Oxford University Press in the UK and in certain other countries

© The Early English Text Society 1876

The moral rights of the authors have been asserted

Database right Oxford University Press (maker)

First Edition published in 1876
Reprinted 1964

All rights reserved. No part of this publication may be reproduced,
stored in a retrieval system, or transmitted, in any form or by any means,
without the prior permission in writing of Oxford University Press,
or as expressly permitted by law, or under terms agreed with the appropriate
reprographics rights organization. Enquiries concerning reproduction
outside the scope of the above should be sent to the Rights Department,
Oxford University Press, at the address above

You must not circulate this book in any other form
and you must impose this same condition on any acquirer

Published in the United States of America by Oxford University Press
198 Madison Avenue, New York, NY 10016, United States of America

British Library Cataloguing in Publication Data
Data available

Library of Congress Cataloging in Publication Data
Data available

Original Series, 65

ISBN 978-0-19-722065-8

PREFACE.

THE poems contained in this volume form part of a MS. in the Library of Corpus Christi College, Cambridge, now numbered CCI., but marked in the old Catalogue and in Wanley as S. 18. The portion of the MS. here printed commences at page 161, and is written in a different hand from that part of the volume which precedes it. A complete list of the contents of this valuable MS. is given in Wanley's Catalogue, pp. 137 seqq., and need not be repeated.

The first two pieces here printed have never been put forth before, with the exception of the few lines given in Wanley, some of which were copied into Conybeare's Illustrations of Anglo-Saxon Poetry (p. lxxx of the introductory Catalogue), but with the mistakes which are in Wanley exactly repeated. Prof. Conybeare had evidently never seen the MS., or he would have given the lines as they are now printed.

In sending forth these texts the sole aim of the Editor has been to put into the reader's hands as complete a representation of the words of the MS. as a printed text can furnish. Either in the text or in the margin the reader will find every letter of the original supplied to him.

Very few notes have been added, but a copious index verborum is appended. This seemed likely to be of more service than notes.

The first of these five poems is an Old English version of what is variously represented as Bede's, or as Alcuin's Latin poem, "De Die Judicii." The Latin text which is herewith printed is taken from the collection of writings attributed to

Bede, and appended to the genuine works of that father published in Migne's Patrologia. But a large portion of the same poem will be found among the works ascribed to Alcuin. In Frobenius' edition of Alcuin, 1777, it is given, with sixteen lines of introduction, at page 616, vol. iii., among the Addenda et Supplenda. The Old English version is of course much later than the date of either of these writers.

The second poem, which the editor has entitled Lár, follows in the MS. immediately after the first, and appears to be an exhortation designed to supplement the former poem.

Wanley has printed the other three poems *in extenso*, and they have been published by Grein among the specimens in his Bibliothek. A few errors which occur in Wanley, and which in some places Grein has emended conjecturally, have been corrected in the present reprint of the poems, and to the whole a rendering in modern English, as literal as was possible, has been supplied.

It will be seen that the poems are defective in many places, as shown by the faulty alliteration in some lines, and here and there by the absence of half a line or more at a time, especially in that curious medley, the Oratio Poetica. The Editor leaves to others the labour of conjectural emendations. He has to thank many friends for suggestions while the sheets have been going through the press, and the authorities of Corpus Christi College for the kindness with which they arranged that he might have access to the MS. To one of their number, the Rev. W. M. Snell, he is also indebted for a careful final reading of the printed text with the MS.

CAMBRIDGE,
Feby. 1876.

CONTENTS.

	PAGES
PREFACE	V–VI

Be Domes Dæge.

Old English Version	2–20
Modern English Version	3–21
Latin Version	22–26

Lay.

Old English Version	28–32
Modern English Version	29–33

Oratio Poetica.

Old English Version	36
Modern English Version	37

Paraphrase of the Lord's Prayer.

Old English Version	40–48
Modern English Version	41–49

Doxology.

Old English Version	52–54
Modern English Version	53–55

NOTES	57–71
INDEX VERBORUM	73–87

Be Domes Dæge.

INCIPIUNT VERSUS BEDÆ PRESBYTERI.
DE DIE JUDICII.

> Inter florigeras fecundi cæspitis herbas
> Flamine ventorum resonantibus undique ramis, etc.

   Hwæt ic ana sæt innan bearwe
   mid helme beþeht· holte tomiddes·
   þær þa wæterburnan swegdon and urnon
4 on middan gehæge· eal swa ic secge·
   eac þær wynwyrta· weoxon and bleowon
   innon þam gemonge on ænlicum wonge·
   and þa wudu-beamas wagedon and swegdon·
8 þurh winda gryre· wolcn wæs gehrered·
   and min earme mod eal wæs gedrefed·
   þa ic færinga· forht and unrot·
   þaf unhýrlican fers· onhéfde mid sange·
12 eall fwylce þu cwæde· synna gemunde·
   lifes leahtra· and þa langan tid·
   þæs dimman cyme· deaðes on eorðan ;
   Ic ondræde me eac· dom þone miclan·
16 for mandædum· mínum on eorðan·
   and þ̅ éce ic éac· yrre ondræde me·
   and synfulra gehwam· æt sylfum gode·
   and hu mihtig frea· eall manna cynn·
20 todæleð and todemeð· þurh his dihlan miht ;
   Ic gemunde eac· mærðe drihtnes·
   and þara haligra on heofonan rice·
   swylce earmsceapenra· yfel[1] and witu ;

[1] MS. yfes.

OF DOOMSDAY.

Lo! I lonely sat within a bower, As I sat in a bower,
With shade bedecked, amidst a wood,
Where the water-burns murmured and ran,
4 Amid an inclosure, all as I say.
There also pleasant plants waxed and bloomed,
Amid the gathering in a peerless meadow;
And the trees of the wood waved and rustled,
8 Through roaring of the winds the welkin was desolated,
And my sad mind was all troubled. my mind was troubled
Then I suddenly, fearful and sad,
This gloomy verse began to sing,
12 All such as thou mayest speak of, mindful of sins, at my sins,
Of the faults of life, and the long tide
Of the coming of dark death on earth. and the coming of death.
I trembled for myself eke at that great doom,
16 For my sinful deeds upon earth.
And I likewise trembled for myself at that eternal ire, I trembled at
And for each sinful one from God himself,
And how the mighty Lord, all men's kin
20 Will sever and doom through his secret might. God's doom, and thought of the blessed and the cursed.
I minded me eke of the glory of the Lord,
And of those holy-ones in heaven's kingdom:
Likewise of the wretched, their evil and punishment.

24 Ic gemunde þis mid me· and ic mearn swiðe·
and ic murcnigende cwæð· mode gedrefed ;
Nu ic eow æddran· ealle bidde·
þ ge wylspringas· wel ontynan·

[1] MS. os.

28 hate on[1] hleorum· recene to tearum·
þænne ic synful slea fwiðe mid fyfte·
breost mine beate· on gebed stowe·
and minne lichaman lecge on eorðan·

32 and gearnade sar ealle ic gecige·
Ic bidde eow benum nuða·
þ ge ne wandian· wiht for tearum·
ac dreorige hleor· dreccað mid wope·

36 and sealtum dropum sona ofer geotaþ·
and geópeniað mán· écum drihtne·
Ne þær owiht inne ne belife
on heort-scræfe· heanra gylta·

40 þ hit ne sy dægcuð· þ þ dihle wæs·
openum wordum· eall abæred·
breoftes· and tungan· and flæsces swa some·
Ðis is an hæl· earmre sauwle·

44 and þam sorgiendum· seleft hihta·

[2] MS. wopa.

þ he wunda her wope[2] gecyðe·
uplicum læce· Se ana mæg.

[3] MS. aglidene gyltas· modgod gode gehælan.

agiltende gyltas· mid gode gehælan·[3]
48 and ræplingaf récene onbindan·
ne mid swiðran his swyþe nele brysan·
wanhydig gemod wealdend engla·
ne þone wlacan smocan· waces flæfcef·

52 wyle waldend crift· wætere gedwæscan·
Hu ne gescéop þe se scaþa· scearplice bysne·
þe mid criste wæs· cwylmed on rode·
hu micel forstent· and hu mære is·

56 feo so e hreow· synna and gylta·
se sceaða wæs on rode· fcyldig and manful·
mid undædum· eall gesymed·

OF DOOMSDAY.

24 I minded this with myself, and I mourned greatly,
And murmuring I spake, troubled in mind.
Now, ye veins, I bid you all   *I bade my*
That ye open well the wellsprings   *tears fall;*
28 Hot on my face quickly for tears.
Then I, sinful, strike strongly with fist,
Beat my breasts in the place of prayer;   *I beat my breasts,*
And my body I lay on the earth,   *and lay on the earth.*
32 And as deserved I invoke all pains.
I bid you now with prayers   *I bid you all*
That ye slack not at all for tears;
But dreary face vex ye with weeping,
36 And with salt drops soon overshed,
And open your sin to the Eternal Lord.
Let there no whit remain within,
In heart cave, of grievous guilts,
40 So that it be not day-clear that which was secret,
With open words all laid bare,
Of breast and tongue and flesh also.
This is only salvation of a poor soul,   *confess your sins to God,*
44 And to the sorrowful best of hopes:
That he his wounds here by weeping make known   *that he may heal you.*
To the leech on high. He only may
The offenders in guilt with good heal,
48 And the prisoners quickly unbind,
He truly will not bruise with his right hand   *He will not bruise you.*
Thoughtless heart, ruler of angels:
Nor the faint smoke of weak flesh
52 Will Christ the ruler with water quench.
Did not the thief warn thee sharply with example,   *Think how the thief on the cross*
Who with Christ was slain on the cross,
How much avails, and how grand is,
56 That true sorrow for sins and offences?
The thief was on the cross, guilty and sinful,
With wrongdoings all laden:

he drihtene swa þeah· deaðe gehende·
60 his bena bebead· breoftgehigdum·
he mid lyt wordum· ac geleaffullum·
his hæle begeat· and help recene
and in-gefor· þa ænlican geatu·
64 neorxnawonges· mid nerigende·
Ic acsige þé la earme geþanc·
hwi lataft þu fwa lange· ꝥ þu ðe læce ne
cyþst·[1]
oððe hwi fwigaft þu· synnigu tunge·
68 nu þu forgifnesse hæfst· gearugne timan·
nu þe ælmihtig· earum atihtum·
heofonrices weard· gehyreð mid luftum·
Ac se dæg cymeð· ðonne demeð god·
72 eorðan ymbhwyrft þu ana scealt·
gyldan scad wordum· wið scyppend god·
and þam rican frean· riht agyldan·
Ic lære ꝥ þu beo hrædra· mid hreowlicum tearum·
76 and ꝥ yrre forfoh· eces deman·
hwæt ligft þu on horwe· leahtrum afylled·
flæsc mid synnum· hwi ne feormast þu·
mid teara gyte· torne synne·
80 hwi ne bidst þu þe beþunga and plafter·
lifes læcedomes· æt lifes frean·
nu þu scealt greotan tearas geotan·
þa hwile tima sy· and tid wopes·
84 nu is halwende· þæt man her wepe·
and dædbote do· drihtne to willan·
Glæd bið se godes sunu· gif þu gnorn þrowast·
and þe sylfum demft· for synnum on eorðan·
88 ne heofenes god· henða and gyltas·
ofer ænne syþ wrecan wile ænigum men;
Ne scealt þu forhyccan· heaf and wopas·
and forgifnesse· gearugne timan·
92 gemyne eac on mode· hu micel is ꝥ wite·

[1] MS. cyftþ.

He to the Lord, nevertheless, nigh unto death,
60 His prayer bade with heart-thoughts: *by prayer gat help,*
He with few words, but full of faith,
His salvation obtained, and help speedily,
And fared in at the peerless gates
64 Of Paradise, with the Redeemer. *and went to Paradise.*
I ask thee, O poor mind,
Why lingerest thou so long, that thou showest not thy-
    self to the leech?
Or why art thou silent, sinful tongue, *Why dost not thou ask forgive-*
68 Now thou for forgiveness hast ready time? *ness now!*
Now thee, the Almighty, with attentive ears,
Ward of heaven's kingdom, will hear with pleasure;
But the day cometh when God will doom
72 The circuit of earth. Thou by thyself shalt
Give account with words to God the Creator,
And to the mighty Lord rightly account.
I rede thee that thou be beforehand with penitent tears,
76 And that anger prevent of the Eternal Judge.
Why liest thou in dust with offences filled,
O Flesh! with sins? Why dost thou not cleanse away, *Why dost thou not cleanse thy*
With flood of tears, grievous sins? *sins with thy tears?*
80 Why askest thou not for thyself bathings and plaster,
Life's leechdoms, of life's Lord?
Now shouldst thou greet, tears pour forth,
While time is, and weeping-tide.
84 Now is it beneficial that man here weep,
And penance do at the Lord's will.
Glad is the Son of God if thou sorrow bearest, *Glad will Christ be of thy sorrow.*
And thyself judgest for sins on earth.
88 Ne'er heaven's God wrongs and guilts
Above one time will wreak on any man;
Nor shouldst thou despise wailing and weeping,
And of forgiveness the ready time.
92 Think also in soul how great is the punishment,

BE DOMES DÆGE.

[1] MS. hit.

[2] MS. sæſ.

[3] MS. geþux-saðˇ.

  þe þara earmra byð· for ærdædum·
  oþþe hu[1] egeſlic· and hu andrysne·
  heah-þrymme cyningc· her wile deman·
96 anra gehwylcum be ærdædum ;
  Oþþe hwylce forebeacn· feran onginnað·
  and criſtes cyme cyþað on eorðan ;
  Eall eorðe bifað· eac swa þa duna
100 dreosað and hreosað·
  and beorga hlida bugað and myltað.
  and se egeslica sweg· ungerydre sǽs[2]
  eall manna mod· miclum gedrefeð
104 eal bið eac upheofon·
  sweart and gesworcen· swiðe gewuxsað·[3]
  deorc and dim hiw· and dwolma sweart·
  þonne stedelease steorran hreosað·
108 and seo sunne forswyrcð· sona on morgen·
  ne se mona næfð nanre mihte wiht·
  ꝥ he þære nihte genipu mæge flecgan·
  eac þonne cumað hider· ufon of heofone
112 deað beacnigende· bregað þa earman ;
  þonne cumað upplice· eored-heapas
  ſtiþ-mægen astyred· ſtyllað embútan·
  eal engla werod ecne behlænað ;
116 Ðone mæran metod· mihte and þrymme ;
  Sitt þonne sigel-beorht· swegles brytta·
  on heah setle· helme beweorðod ;
  We beoð færinga· him beforan brohte·
120 æghwanum cumene· to his ansyne·
  That gehwilc underfó dom be his dædum· æt drihtne sylfum ;
  Ic bidde man that þu gemune· hu micel bið se broga
  beforan domsetle drihtneſ þænne·
124 stent he heortleas· and earh·
  amasod· and amarod· mihtleas· afæred·

OF DOOMSDAY.

    That to the wretched shall be for former sins.
    Either how aweful and how dreadful   *Think of God's Judgement Day,*
    A King in his majesty here will judge
96 Each man by his former deeds.
    Or what tokens begin to fare,   *and the tokens that come before it.*
    And Christ's coming show on earth.
    Earth all shaketh, and likewise the mountains
100 Perish and fall,
    And the doors of the graves bend and melt;   *The graves shall open,*
    And the fearful noise of the boisterous sea
    All men's hearts much affrighteth,
104 Utterly also is heaven above
    Swart and cloudy, quickly it waxeth
    Dark and dim-hued, and a swart chaos.
    Then stedless stars fall,   *the stars shall fall.*
108 And the sun grows dark early in the day,
    Nor has the moon aught of any might
    That she the night's clouds may disperse.
    Also then shall come hither, down from heaven,
112 Death-tokenings, affright the miserable:
    Then shall come on high mighty hosts,   *Then, with hosts of angels, shall God come,*
    A strong power stirred they hurry around.
    The hosts of all angels surround the Eternal
116 The great Creator, with might and host.
    There shall sit, sun-bright, the firmament's ruler
    On high throne with crown honoured,
    We shall be suddenly brought before him,   *and we shall*
120 From all sides coming to his presence;
    That each may receive doom for his deeds from the *be doomed.*
        Lord himself.
    I bid, O man, that thou remember how great will
        be the terror
    Before the Lord's judgment-seat then.
124 He stands heartless and timorous,
    Amazed and disturbed, powerless, terrified;

BE DOMES DÆGE.

[1] MS. sweges.
[2] MS. eorbuen-dra.
[3] MS. eeal.
[4] MS. eah.

þænne samod becumaðˑ of swegles[1] hleoˑ
eall engla werodˑ ecne ymtrymmað.
128 æne bið geban micelˑ and aboden þiderˑ
eal adames cnoslˑ eorðbuendra[2]
þe on foldan wearðˑ fedend æfreˑ
oððe modar gebærˑ to manlicanˑ
132 oþþe þa þe wæronˑ oððe woldon beonˑ
oþþe to-weardeˑ geteald wæron awiht;
Ðonne eallum beoð ealra gesweotoludeˑ
digle geþancasˑ on þære dægtideˑ
136 eal ꝥ seo heorteˑ hearmeſ geþohteˑ
oððe seo tunge to teonan geclypedeˑ
oþþe mannes handˑ manes gefremedeˑ
on þystrum scræfumˑ þinga on eorðanˑ
140 eal ꝥ hwæne sceamodeˑ scylda on worulde.
ꝥ he ænigum men. ypte. oððe cyðde;
þonne bið eallum openˑ æt somne
gelíceˑ alyfed ꝥ man lange hæl;
144 Ufenan eall þis eac byð gefylled
eal uplic lyftˑ ættrenum ligeˑ
færð fýr ofer eallˑ ne byð þær nan forestealˑ
ne him man nane mæg miht forwyrnan;
148 eal[3] ꝥ us þincð æmtig eac[4] gemearcesˑ
under roderes ryneˑ readum lige
bið emnes mid þyˑ eal gefylled;
Ðonne fyren lig blawað and braslað.
152 read and reaðeˑ ræsct and efesteðˑ
hu he synfullum susle gefremedeˑ
Ne se wrecenda brynæˑ wile forbuganˑ
oððe ænigum þærˑ are gefremmanˑ
156 buton he horwum syˑ her afeormadˑ
and þonne þider cumeˑ þearle aclænsad;
þonne fela mægða· folca unrim
heora sinnigan breostˑ swiðlice beataðˑ
160 forhte mid fysteˑ for fyren-lustum;

OF DOOMSDAY.

    Then together will come from the firmament's shade
    All the hosts of angels, the Eternal surround.
128 At once will be a loud proclamation, and called thither   *All Adam's race*
    All Adam's race, of earth inhabitants,   *shall appear,*
    That on earth have been supported ever,
    Or mother bare in human form,
132 Or those that were or should be,
    Or who were at all about to be reckoned.
    Then to all will be of all disclosed   *all secrets shall*
    The secret thoughts, on the day-tide,   *be known,*
136 All that the heart of harm devised,
    Or the tongue for injustice spake,
    Or man's hand of evil framed,
    In dark caves, of things on earth ;
140 All that any one shamed of sins in the world   *and all shames.*
    That he to any man should open or tell,
    Then will be to all open altogether,
    Alike set free that man long hid.
144 Beside all this, also will be filled
    All the lofty lift with poisonous fire.
    Fire will fare over all, nor will be there any hindrance :   *Fire will be over all,*
    Nor himself by any means may man forewarn.
148 All that we think empty also of boundary,
    Under the roaring of the sky with red blaze,
    Will be all alike therewith utterly filled.
    Then the flame of the fire will blow and crackle,
152 Red and angry, will rush and hurry
    How it for the sinful torture might prepare.   *and torture all*
    Nor will the punishing flame forbear,
    Or towards any there act with favour ;
156 Unless he be here from filth cleansed,   *who are not cleansed from*
    And then thither come throughly clean.   *sin.*
    Then many races, of folks without number,
    Their sinful breasts strongly will beat,
160 Fiercely with fist, for their gross luxury.

BE DOMES DÆGE.

  þær beoð þearfan and þeod-cyningas·
  earm and eadig ealle beoð afæred·
  þær hæfð ane lage earm and se welega.
164 forðon hi habbað ege· ealle ætsomne;
  Dæt reðe flod ræscet fyre·
  and biterlice bærnð· ða earman saula·
  and heora heortan· horxlice wyrmas·
168 sýn scýldigra· ceorfað and slitað·
  ne mæg þær æniman· be arnum gewyrhtum·
  gedyrstig wesan·[1] deman gehende·
  ac ealle þurh yrnð óga æt somne.[2]
172 breost gehyda· and se bitera wóp·
  and þær stænt astifad· stane gelicast·
  eal arleas heap· yfelef on wenan ;
  hwæt dest þu la flæsc· hwæt dreogeft þu nú·
176 hwæt miht þu on þa tid þearfe gewepan ;
  Wa þe nu þu þeowast·
  and her glæd leofast. on galnysse
  and þe mid stiðum astyrest· sticelum þær gælsan ;
180 Hwi ne forhtað þu fyrene egsan·
  and þe sylfum ondræd· swiðlice witu·
  ða deoflum geo drihten geteode·
  awyrgedum gastum weana to leane·
184 þa oferswiðað· sefan and spræce·
  Manna gehwylces for micelnysse
  nænig spræc mæg beon· spellum areccan·
  ænegum on eorðan· earmlice witu·
188 fule stowa fyres on grunde·
  þe wæs in grimmum susle on helle ;
  þær fynt to sorge æt somne gemenged·
  se þrosma lig· and se þrece gicela
192 swiðe hat and ceald· helle to middes·
  hwilum þær éagan ungemetum wepað·
  for þæs ofnes bryne· eal he is bealuwes full ;
  hwilum eac þa teþ for miclum cyle manna þær gryrrað ;

[1] MS. weran.
[2] MS. sóne.

OF DOOMSDAY.

    There will be the needy, and kings of people,
    Poor and rich all will be affrighted.
    There will have one law, poor and the wealthy.   *Rich and poor will be judged alike.*
164 Therefore they will have fear all alike.
    That angry flood will rush with fire,
    And bitterly burn the poor souls:
    And the hearts, savagely worms,
168 Of sin-guilty ones, will carve and tear.
    Nor may there any man, by works of merit,
    Bold become in presence of the Judge;
    But terror will run alike through all,   *All will be terrified.*
172 Thoughts of the heart, and the bitter weeping.
    And there will stand, stiffened most like to stone,
    All the wicked troop, in expectation of evil.
    What doest thou, O flesh? what actest thou now?   *Flesh, thou*
176 How might thou on that tide bewail thy trouble?
    Woe! thou servest now thyself,
    And here gladly livest in lust,   *livest now in lust.*
    And thyself with keen goads there urgest to luxury.
180 Why wilt thou not fear the fiery terror,   *Wilt thou not fear hell,*
    And for thyself dread greatly the punishments
    Which for devils of yore the Lord prepared
    To cursed souls for wages of woe?
184 These overpass thought and speech,
    Of every man for greatness.
    No speech may be with tidings to recount
    To any on earth the wretched penalties,
188 Filthy places of fire in the depth,   *fire and sulphur,*
    That was mid fierce torment in hell.
    There be for sorrow together mingled
    The flame of vapours, and the weariness of cold,   *vapour and cold?*
192 Very heat and cold, in midst of hell.
    One while there the eyes without measure will weep;
    For the scorching of the furnace, he is all full of misery;
    One while too the teeth of men for great cold there
        will gnash.

BE DOMES DÆGE.

<small>¹ MS. þromes.</small>

<small>² MS. unftence.</small>

<small>³ MS. grisgbig-tung.</small>

196 þis atule gewrixl· earmsceape men·
  on worulda woruld· wendað þær inne·
  betwyx forsworcenum sweartum nihtum·
  and weallendes pices· wean & þrosmes¹
200 þær nan stefne styreð butan stearc-heard
  wop· and wanung na-wiht elles·
  ne bið þær ánsyn gesewen. ænigre wihte·
  butan þara cwelra becwylmað ða earman·
204 ne bið þær ínne áht geméted·
  butan líg· and cyle· and laðlic fúl
  hy mid nósan ne magon naht geswæccan·
  butan unftences² ormætneffe·
208 þær beoð þa wanigendran· welras gefylde·
  ligspiwelum bryne· laðlices fyres
  and hy wæl-grimme· wyrmas slitað
  and heora ban gnagað. brynigum tuxlum.
212 Ufenon eal þis bið ꝥ earme breost·
  mid bitere care breged and swenced.
  for hwi fyrgende flæsc· on þas frecnan tid
  hym selfum swa fela synna· geworhte·
216 ꝥ hit on cweartern cwylmed wyrde·
  þær ða atelan synd· ecan witu·
  þær leohtef ne leoht lytel sperca·
  earmum ænig· ne þær arfæstnes·
220 ne sib· ne hópa· ne swige· gegladað·
  ne þara wera worn wihte·
  Flyhð frofor aweg ne bið þær fultum nan·
  ꝥ wið þa biteran þing· gebeorh mæge fremman ;
224 Ne bið þær ansyn gemet· ænigre blisse·
  ꝥ bið angryslic· ege & fyrhtu·
  and sarimod swiðlic· gristbitung³
  þær bið unrotnes æghwær wæl-hreow
228 eald· and yrre· and æmelnes
  and þær synne eac. sauwle on lige·
  on blindum fcræfe· byrnað & yrnað ;

OF DOOMSDAY.

196 This foul vicissitude, miserable men,
    For ever and ever, will wend therein :
    Amid dark black night
    And the woe of boiling pitch and vapour.
200 There no sound stirroth, save stark laid   *Naught is heard but weeping and woe,*
    Weeping and lamenting, naught else.
    Nor will be any appearance seen of any wight,
    But of the torturers (which) punish the miserable.
204 Nor will there be therein aught found   *naught smelt but stench.*
    But fire, and cold, and loathsome filth.
    They with nose may naught smell
    Save immensity of stench.
208 There will be the wretched lips filled
    With flame-vomiting blaze of loathly fire,
    And the cruel worms will tear them,
    And will gnaw their bones with burning tusks.
212 Above all this will be that wretched breast
    With bitter care frightened and troubled.
    For why luxurious flesh in the perilous tide
    For himself so many sins wrought,
216 That it in prison became destroyed ;
    There are the dreadful everlasting punishments,
    There not any little spark of light shineth
    To the miserable. There neither goodness
220 Nor peace, nor hope, nor quiet delighteth,   *There is neither peace nor hope,*
    Nor the number of the men at all.
    Consolation will fly away, nor will there be any help
    That against the bitter circumstances may frame a protection :
224 Nor will there appearance be found of any bliss :   *but terror,*
    There will be horrid fear and terror,
    And violent sorrowful gnashing of teeth.   *sadness,*
    There will be everywhere cruel sadness,
228 Eld and anger and weariness,   *and sin.*
    And there too sin. Souls in fire
    In the dark cave will burn and wander.

BE DOMES DÆGE.

<blockquote>

þonne deriende gedwinað heonone·
232 þyſſe worulde geféan. gewítað mid ealle·
þonne druncennes· gedwineð mid wiſtum·
and hleahter· and plega· hleapað æt somne·
and wrænnes eac· gewiteð heonone·
236 and fæſthafolnes· feor gewiteð·
uncyſt on-weg· & ælc gælsa·
ſcyldig ſcyndan·[1] on sceade þone·
& ſe earma flyhð· uncræftiga ſlæp·
240 fléac mid sluman· flincan on hinder;
Ðonne blindum beseah· biterum ligum·
earme on ende. ꝥ unalyfed iſ nu·
leofeſt[2] on life· lað bið þænne·
244 and ꝥ werige mod wendað þa gyltaſ.
ſwiðe mid sorgum· and mid sargunge·
Eala ſe bið gesælig and ofer sælig.
& on worulda woruld· wihta[3] gesæligoſt·
248 ſe þe mid gesyntum· ſwylce cwyldas·
and witum mæg· wel forbugon·
and samod blíðe· on woruld ealle·
hiſ þeodne geþeon· & þonne mot habban
252 heofonrice· ꝥ is hihta mæſt·
þær niht ne genipð· næfre þeostra·
þæs heofenlican leohtes sciman·
ne cymð þær sorh ne sár· ne gefwenced yld·
256 ne þær ænig gefwinc· æfre gelimpeð·
oððe hunger· oððe þurst· oððe heanlic slæp·
ne bið þær fefur· ne adl· ne færlic cwyld·
naneſ liges gebrasl· ne se laðlica cyle·
260 nis þær unrotnes· ne þær æmelnys·
ne hryre· ne caru· ne hreoh tintrega·
ne bið þær liget. ne laðlic storm·
winter· ne þunerrad· ne wiht cealdes·
264 ne þær hagul ſcuras hearde mid snawe[4]
ne bið þær wædl· ne lyre· ne deaðes **gryre**·

</blockquote>

[1] MS. scyndam.

[2] MS. leofes.

[3] MS. wihtna.

[4] MS. swa se.

OF DOOMSDAY.

  Then will perish from hence the fatal
232 Joys of this world; they will depart all together.   *Worldly joys there vanish,*
  Then drunkenness will cease with feasts,
  And laughter and play will leap together.
  And lust also will depart hence,
236 And greed will far depart,
  Wickedness away, and each luxury,
  Guilty to hasten into the shade.
  And the wretched helpless sleep will fly,
240 Slack with slumber, to slink behind.
  Then in dark bitter fire saw
  The poor at last, that which forbidden is now;
  That most loved in life, loathed will be then,   *and the desire of life be loathed.*
244 And the guilts will turn that weary heart
  Verily among sorrows and among misery.
  Oh! he will be happy, and more than happy,   *Happy will be he who with*
  And world-without-end of men the happiest,
248 He that with prosperity, such overthrow,
  And with understanding, may well escape,   *wit escapes this hell,*
  And likewise blessed in all the world
  Serve his lord, and then may have
252 Heaven's kingdom, that is of joys the best.   *and gains God's heaven,*
  There night nor darkness overclouds
  The sheen of heavenly light.
  There cometh not sorrow nor pain, nor toilworn eld,   *where comes not sorrow or pain,*
256 Nor happeth there ever any toil;
  Either hunger, or thirst, or miserable sleep.
  There is not fever, nor decay, nor sudden plague,
  Crackling of no fire, nor the loathsome cold,
260 There is not mourning, nor there weariness,   *mourning or care,*
  Nor ruin, nor care, nor fierce torment.
  Nor is there lightning, nor loathsome storm,
  Winter, nor thunder shower, nor a whit of cold;
264 Nor there are mighty hail-showers with snow,
  Nor is want there, nor loss, nor terror of death,   *want, or death.*

BE DOMES DÆGE.

    ne yrmð· ne agnes· ne nænigu gnornung
    Ac þær samod ricxað· sib mid spede·
268 and arfæstnes· and ece god·
    wuldor· and wurðmynt·
    swylce lof· and lif· and leoflic geþwærnes·[1]
    Ufenan eal þis éce drihten him ealra
272 goda gehwylc· glædlice ðenað ;
    þæra andweard ealle weorðaþ and fehþ·
    and geblyfað fæder ætsomne· wuldraþ and wel hylt·
    fægere frætuað· and freolice lufað·
276 & in heofon-fetle· heah gehrineð·[2]
    his sunu bliðe· sigores brytta·
    fylð anragehwam· ece mede·
    heofonlice hyrfta· þ is healic gifu·
280 gemang þam ænlican engla werode·
    and þæra haligra heapum and þreatum[3]
    þær hy beoð geþeode þeodfcipum on gemang·
    betwyx heahfæderas· and halige witegan·
284 blissiendum modum· byrgum to middes·
    þær þa ærendracan synd· ælmihtiges godes·
    and betweoh rofena reade heapaf·
    þær symle scinað·
288 þær þæra hwittra hwyrfð mæden-heap·
    bloftmum behangen· beortost wereda
    þe ealle læt ænlicu godes drut·
    feo frowe þe us frean acende·
292 metod on moldan· meowle seo clæne·
    þæt is MARÍA· mædena felast·
    heo let þurh þa scenan scinendan rícu·
    gebletsodost ealra. þæs breman fæder·
296 betweox fæder and sunu· freolicum werede·
    and betwyx þære écan uplicum sibbe·
    rice rædwitan rodera-weardes;[4]
    hwæt mæg beon heardes her on life·

[1] gehþwærnes MS.
[2] MS. hean gerinnað.
[3] þreapum MS.
[4] MS. weardas.

OF DOOMSDAY.

Nor misery, nor sorrow, nor any mourning.
But there together reigneth peace with prosperity,   *But ever peace*
268 And virtue, and eternal good,
Glory and honour,
Likewise praise, and life, and faithful concord.
Beside all this the Eternal Lord to them of all
272 Goods any gladly serveth,
And in presence honoureth and receiveth all of them ;
And the Father likewise blesseth, glorifieth, and well-   *the blessing of God,*
regardeth (them),
Beautifully decks, and liberally loveth,
276 And on heaven's throne on high adorneth.
His kind Son, lord of Victory,   *the gift of Christ,*
Gives to each one everlasting meed,
Heavenly glories, that is a splendid gift.
    the fellowship of angels,
280 Among the beautiful host of angels,
And in troops and throngs of the holy ones,
There shall they be associated among nations,
Amidst the patriarchs and holy prophets.
284 In blissful mood among the cities,
There be the apostles of Almighty God.
And amid the stores of roses red
There ever shall they shine.
288 There of the white ones shall wander a maiden throng   *the company of virgins,*
With blossoms hung. Brightest of the hosts,
Who them all will lead, God's peerless dear one,   *led by*
The woman who for us the Lord conceived,
292 Creator on earth : virgin the pure,
That is MARY, of maidens most blessed.   *Mary, mother of God.*
She will lead through those bright shining kingdoms
(Blessedest she of all) of the glorious father,
296 Betwixt father and son, a goodly host,
And mid eternal heavenly peace,
In the kingdom of the wise heavenly ruler.
What of hardship can there be here in life,   *What are earth's hardships to this?*

300 Gif þu wille secgan soð þæm ðe frineð·
    wið þam þu mote· gemang þam werode·
    eardian unbleoh· on ecnesse·
    and on upcundra· eadegum setlum·
304 brucan bliðnesse butan ende forð·

Her endað þeof boc þe hatte inter florigeras ðæt is on englisc betwyx blowende þe to godes rice farað. and hu ða þrowiað þe to helle farað.

300 If thou wilt say sooth to him that asketh thee   <small>Thou mayst live in bliss without an end.</small>
    To set against this, that thou mayest, among that host,
    Live unchanging through eternity,
    And in the happy seats of the saints above
304 Enjoy bliss henceforth without end.

Here endeth this book that is called inter florigeras, *that is, in English, "betwixt blooming," who to God's Kingdom fare: and how those suffer, who to Hell fare.*

DE DIE JUDICII.

[From Migne's Edition of BEDE, Vol. V. p. 634.]

Inter florigeras fecundi cespitis herbas,
Flamine ventorum resonantibus undique ramis,
Arboris umbriferæ mæstus sub tegmine solus
4 Dum sedi, subito planctu turbatus amaro,
Carmina præ tristi cecini hæc lugubria mente
Utpote commemorans scelerum commissa meorum,
Et maculas vitæ, mortisque inamabile tempus,
8 Judiciique diem horrendo examine magnum,
Perpetuamque reis districti judicis iram,
Et genus humanum discretis sedibus omne,
Gaudia sanctorum necnon, poenasque malorum.
12 Hæc memorans mecum tacito sub murmure dixi :
Nunc rogo, nunc venæ fontes aperite calentes,
Dumque ego percutiam pugnis rea pectora, vel dum
Membra solo sternam, meritosque ciebo dolores,
16 Vos, precor, effusis lacrymis non parcite statim,
Sed mœstam salsis faciem perfundite guttis.
Et reserate nefas Christo cum voce gementi,
Nec lateat quidquam culparum cordis in antro.
20 Omnia quin luci verbis reddantur apertis,
Pectoris et linguæ, carnis vel crimina sæva.
Hæc est sola salus animæ, et spes certa dolenti,
Vulnera cum lacrymis medico reserare superno;

24 Qui solet allisos sanare et solvere vinctos,
   Quassatos nec vult calamos infringere dextra
   Nec lini tepidos undis exstinguere fumos.
   Nonne exempla tibi pendens dabat in cruce latro
28 Peccati quantum valeat confessio vera?
   Qui fuit usque crucem sceleratis impius actis,
   Mortis in articulo sed verba precantia clamat,
   Et solo meruit fidei sermone salutem,
32 Cum Christo et portas paradisi intravit apertas.
   Cur rogo, mens, tardas medico te pandere totam?
   Vel cur lingua, taces, veniæ dum tempus habebis?
   Auribus Omnipotens te nunc exaudit apertis.
36 Ille dies veniet, judex dum venerit orbis
   Debebis qua tu rationem reddere de te.
   Suadeo prævenias lacrymis modo judicis iram.
   Quid tu in sorde jaces, scelerum caro plena piaclis?
40 Cur tua non purgas lacrymis peccata profusis
   Et tibi non oras placidæ fomenta medelæ?
   Fletibus assiduis est dum data gratia flendi,
   Pœnituisse juvat tibi nunc et flere salubre est.
44 Æternus fuerit placidus te vindice judex.
   Nec Deus ætherius bis crimina vindicat ulli,
   Spernere tu noli veniæ tibi tempora certa.
   Quanta malis maneant etiam tormenta memento,
48 Vel quam celsithronus metuendus ab arce polorum
   Adveniet judex, mercedem reddere cunctis,
   Præcurrent illum vel qualia signa, repente
   Terra tremet, montesque ruent, collesque liquescent
52 Et mare terribili confundet murmure mentes.
   Tristius et cœlum tenebris obducitur atris,
   Astra cadunt rutilo et Titan tenebrescit in ortu.
   Pallida nocturnam nec præstat luna lucernam,
56 De cœlo venient et signa minantia mortem,
   Tum superum subito veniet commota potestas,
   Cœtibus angelicis regem stipata supernum.

Ille sedens solio fulget sublimis in alto,
60 Ante illum rapimur, collectis undique turmis,
Judicium ut capiat gestorum quisque suorum.
Sis memor illius, qui tum pavor ante tribunal
Percutiet stupidis cunctorum corda querelis.
64 Dum simul innumeris regem comitata polorum
Angelica advenient coelestibus agmina turmis,
Atque omnes pariter homines cogentur adesse,
Qui sunt, qui fuerant, fuerint vel quique futuri
68 Cunctaque cunctorum cunctis arcana patebunt.
Quod cor, lingua, manus tenebrosis gessit in antris
Et quod nunc aliquem verecundans scire veretur
Omnibus in patulo pariter tunc scire licebit.
72 Insuper impletur flammis altricibus aer,
Ignis ubique suis ruptis regnabit habenis.
Et quo nunc aer gremium diffundit inane
Ignea tunc sonitus perfundet flamma feroces,
76 Festinans scelerum sævas ulciscere causas.
Nec vindex ardor cuiquam tunc parcere curat,
Sordibus ablutus veniat nisi ab omnibus illuc.
Tunc tribus et populi ferient rea pectora pugnis
80 Stabit uterque simul stupidus, pauperque potensque
Et miser et dives simili ditione timebunt:
Fluvius ignivomus miseros torquebit amare
Et vermes scelerum mordebunt intima cordis.
84 Nullus ibi meritis confidit judice præsens,
Singula sed nimius percurrit pectora terror
Et stupet attonito simul impia turba timore.
Quid, caro, quid facies, illâ quid flebilis horâ
88 Quæ modo væ misera servire libidine gaudes,
Luxuriæque tuæ stimulis te agitabis acutis
Ignea tu tibimet cur non tormenta timebis,
Dæmonibus dudum fuerantque parata malignis.
92 Quæ superant sensus cunctorum et dicta virorum,
Nec vox ulla valet miseras edicere pœnas,

Ignibus æternæ nigris loca plena gehennæ,
Frigora mista simul ferventibus algida flammis
96 Nunc oculos nimio flentes ardore camini
Nunc iterum nimio stridentes frigore dentes.
His miseris vicibus miseri volvuntur in ævum
Obscuras inter picea caligine noctes.
100 Vox ubi nulla sonat, durus nisi fletus ubique,
Non nisi tortorum facies ubi cernitur ulla.
Non sentitur ibi quidquam nisi frigora, flammæ
Fœtor et ingenti complet putredine nares.
104 Os quoque flammivomum lugens implebitur igne,
Et vermes lacerant ignitis dentibus ossa.
Insuper et pectus curis torquetur amaris,
Cur caro luxurians sibimet sub tempore parvo
108 Atro perpetuas meruisset carcere pœnas,
Lucis ubi miseris nulla scintilla relucet
Nec pax nec pietas immo spes nulla quietis
Flentibus arrident, fugiunt solatia cuncta.
112 Auxilium nullus rebus præstabit amaris,
Lætitiæ facies jam nulla videbitur illic
Sed dolor et gemitus, stridor, pavor, et timor horrens,
Tædia, tristitiæ, trux indignatio, languor.
116 Errantesque animæ flammis in carcere cæco.
Noxia tunc hujus cessabunt gaudia sæcli,
Ebrietas, epulæ, risus, petulantia, jocus,
Dira cupido, tenax luxus, scelerata libido,
120 Somnus iners torporque gravis, desidia pigra
Illicitat quidquid modo delectatio carnis
Et cæca scelerum mergit vertigine mentem,
Tunc cæcis merget flammis sine fine misellos.
124 Felix o nimium, semperque in sæcula felix
Qui illas effugiet pœnarum prospere clades
Cum sanctisque simul lætatur in omnia sæcla!
Conjunctus Christo cœlestia regna tenebit,
128 Nox ubi nulla rapit splendorem lucis amœnæ,

Non dolor aut gemitus veniet, nec fessa senectus
Non sitis, esuries, somnus et non labor ullus
Non febris, morbi, clades, non frigora, flammæ
132 Tædia, tristitiæ, curæ, tormenta, ruinæ
Fulmina, nimbus, hiems, tonitru, nix, grando, procella,
Angor, paupertas, mœror, mors, casus, egestas,
Sex pax et pietas, bonitas, opulentia regnat,
136 Gaudia, lætitiæ, virtus, lux, vita perennis
Gloria, laus, requies, honor et concordia dulcis,
Insuper omne bonum cunctis Deus ipse ministrat.
Semper adest præsens, cunctos fovet, implet, honorat,
140 Glorificat, servat, veneratur, diligit, ornat,
Collocat Altithrono, lætosque in sede polorum
Præmia perpetuis tradens cœlestia donis.
Angelicas inter turmas sanctasque cohortes
144 Vatidicis junctos patriarchis atque prophetis
Inter apostolicas animis lætantibus arces.
Atque inter roseis splendentia castra triumphis
Candida virgineo simul inter agmina flore.
148 Quæ trahit alma Dei genetrix, pia Virgo Maria,
Per benedicta Patris fulgenti regna paratu
Inter et Ecclesiæ sanctos, natosque, patresque,
Inter et ætherium cœlesti pace senatum.
152 Quid, rogo, quid durum, sæclo consetur in isto,
Utque illas inter liceat habitare cohortes,
Sedibus et superum semper gaudere beatis?
Incolumem mihi te Christi charissima proles,
156 Protegat, et faciat semper sine fine beatam
Meque tuis Christo precibus commenda benignis.

Lár.

(AN EXHORTATION.)

LÁR.

[Immediately after the previous version, the MS. has the following lines.]

Nu lære ic þe fwa man leofne fceal·
gif þu wille that blowende ríce gestigan·
þænne beo þu eadmod· & ælmes georn·
4 wis on wordum· and wæccan lufa·
on hyge halgum. on þas hwilwendan tid·
bliðe mode· and gebedum filige·
oftost symle· þær þu ana sy·
8 forðan ꝥ halige gebed· and seo hluttre lufu·
godes and manna. and seo ælmes sylen· and se miccla hopa
to þinum hælende· ꝥ he þine fynna
adwæfcan wylle· and eac oþera fela
12 godra weorca· glengað and bringað.
þa soðfæstan sauwle to reste.
on þa uplican eadignesse·
Wyrc ꝥ þu wyrce· word oððe dæda·
16 hafa metodes ege· on gemang fymle·
ꝥ is witodlice wisdomes ord·
ꝥ þu ꝥ ece leoht· eal ne forleose·
þeos woruld is æt ende· and we synd wædlan gýt·
20 heofena rices· ꝥ is hefig byrdæn.
and þeah þu æfter þinum ende eall gesylle·
ꝥ þu on eorðan ær gestryndes·
goda gehwylces· wylle gode cweman·
24 ne mihtu mid þæm eallum· saule þine

EXHORTATION.

Now I teach thee as one shall do a beloved one.
If thou wilt attain that blooming realm,   *If thou wilt heaven win,*
Then be thou humble, and bountiful,
4 Wise in words, and love watchfulness.
In holy thought, in the present time,   *be holy, kind, and pray.*
Kind of disposition, and abundant in prayers,
Continually when thou art alone.
8 Because holy prayer, and pure love
Of God and man, and almsgiving, and the great trust
In thy Saviour, that he thy sins
Will erase, and likewise many other
12 Good works adorn and bring
The upright soul to rest
In heavenly happiness.
Work what thou workest, word or deed;   *Work; fear God.*
16 Have fear of the Creator, in the midst,
That is assuredly the beginning of wisdom,
That thou the everlasting light all do not lose.
This world is fleeting, and we are yet poor
20 Of heaven's kingdom. That is a heavy burden.
And though thou after thine end give everything   *Trust not to death-bed alms.*
That thou on earth before acquiredst
Of each good, will it please God?
24 Nor might thou, with the whole, thy soul

ut alyfan gif heo inne wyrð
feondum befangen· frofre bedæled·
welena forwynned· ac þu wuldres god·
28 éce ælmihtigne· ealninga bidde·
ꝥ he þe ne forlæte· laðum to handa·
feondum to frofre· ac þu fleoh þanan·
syle ælmesfan. oft and gelome.
32 digolice ꝥ bið drihtnes lár·
gumena gehwylcef· þe on god gelyfð ;
Ceapa þe mid æhtum eces leohtes·
þy læs þu forweorðe· þænne þu hyra geweald
36 nafast to syllanne· hit bið swiðe yfel
manna gehwilcum· ꝥ he micel age·
gif he him god ne ondræt·
fwiðor micle· þonne his sylfes gewil·
40 Warna þe georne wið þære wambe fylle·
forþan heo þa unþeawaf ealle gesomnað·
þe þære saule fwiðoft deriað·
ꝥ if druncennef· and dyrne geligere·
44 ungemet wilnung. ætef· & flæpef·
þa man mæg mid fæftenum·
and forhæfdnessum heonon adrifan·
and mid cyric focnum cealdum wederum·
48 eadmodlice· ealluncga biddan·
heófena drihten· ꝥ he þe hǽl gife.
milde mund bora· fwa him gemet þince·
and ondræd þu ðe dihle wifan·
52 nearwe geþancaf· þe on niht becumað·
fyn luftaf for-oft· fwiðe fremman·
earfoðlice· þy þu earhlice fcealt·
gyltas þine· fwiðe bemurnan.
56 har hilderinc· hefie þe ðincaþ·
fynna þine· forþam þu sylf ongýte·
ꝥ þu alætan scealt· læne fcaþelaf·

EXHORTATION.

  Release, if it become among   They will not
  Fiends captured, of comfort bereft,   friends.
  Of wealth deprived. But do thou the God of glory,
28 The eternal almighty, constantly pray   Pray;
  That he let thee not fall into the hands of evil ones,
  To the gain of fiends. But flee thou from thence,
  Give alms, oft and repeatedly, in secret,   give alms oft in
                    thy life;
32 That is the exhortation of the Lord,
  For each man that believes in God.
  Buy for thyself eternal light with thy possessions, buy thyself
                    heaven with thy
  The less wilt thou be undone, when thou the power goods on earth.
    over them
36 Hast not to give. It is very evil
  To every man that he have much,
  If he fear not God
  Much more than his own will.
40 Take thou good heed against gluttony,   Guard against
  For it assembleth all the bad qualities   gluttony.
  Which most destroy the soul,
  That is, drunkenness and secret fornication,
44 Undue longing for food and sleep.
  These man may with fasting   Drive it off with
                     fasting, and
  And continence drive away,   church-going in
                     the cold.
  And with church going in cold weather.
48 Humbly always [take care] to pray
  The Lord of heaven, that he give thee health,
  The kind protector, as to him seems fit;
  And be thou afraid of secret plans,   Fear too bad
                     thoughts at
52 Of troublesome thoughts, that arise at night,   night.
  Sinful desires oftentimes greatly to produce.
  With trouble therefore thou in terror shalt
  Thy offences greatly mourn.
56 Grey-haired warrior, heavy seem to thee
  Thy sins. Therefore do thou thyself understand
  That thou shalt leave thy gifts unharmed,

eard. and eþel· uncuð bið þe þænne·
60 to hwan þe þin drihten gedon wille·
þænne þu lengc ne moſt· lifeſ brucan·
eardes on eþle· swa þu ær dydest·
blissum hremi· nu þu ðe beorgan scealt·
64 and wið feonda gehwæne· fæſte healdan·
ſauwle þine· á hi winnað embe
[1] dæges & nihtes· ongean drihtnes líf;
þú miht hy gefleman gif þu filian wilt·
68 larum minum. swa ic lære þe
digollice· ꝥ þu on dægred·
oft ymbe þynre sauwle ræd· swiðe smeage·
hu þu ꝥ ece leoht. æfre begytan mæge.
72 síðe geſécan· þu fcealt glædlice· ſwiðe ſwincan·
wið þæs úplican· éþelríceſ·
dægeſ & nihteſ· þu scealt drúncen fleon·
and þa oferfylle· ealle forlætan·
76 gif þu wilt þa úpplican eárdwic ceosan·
þænne ſcealt þu hit on eórðan ǽr geþencan·
and þu þe ſylfne· ſwiðe gebinde·
and þa unþeawaſ· ealle forlætan·
80 þe þu on þiſ life· ær lufedest & feddest·

[1] ꝥ added in MS.

EXHORTATION.

    Land and country. Unknown to thee then will be
60 Whither thy lord will assign thee;
    When thou no longer mayest enjoy life   *Thou canst not live long.*
    In earth's region, as thou didst before
    Exulting in bliss. Now oughtest thou to save thyself, *Save thyself then!*
64 And against every enemy hold fast
    Thy soul. Ever they labour around,
    By day and night, against the lord's life.
    Thou mightest put them to flight, if thou wilt follow   *Rout thy soul's foes!*
68 My teaching, as I teach thee—
    Secretly that thou in the early morn
    Oft for thy soul's advantage earnestly meditate
    How thou the eternal light ever mayest attain;
72 With pains to seek, thou shalt gladly eagerly labour   *Seek the kingdom of heaven.*
    After the heavenly kingdom;
    By day and night, thou shalt drunkenness flee,   *Flee drunkenness, gluttony,*
    And gluttony all forego.
76 If thou wilt that heavenly land choose,
    Then shalt thou on earth before think on it,
    And earnestly restrain thyself,
    And forego all bad habits   *and all thy old bad habits.*
80 Which thou in life formerly didst love and cherish.

Oratio Poetica.

ORATIO POETICA.

     Thænne gemiltsað þe· N. mundum qui regit·
¹ MS. seden- ðeoda þrym-Cyningc· Thronum sedens¹
tem.   a butan ende·
    4 saule wine·
     Geunne þe on life· Auctor pacis·
     Sibbe gesælða· salus mundi·
     metod se mæra· magna virtute·
    8 & se soðfæsta· summi filius·
     fo on fultum· factor cosmi·
     se of æðelre wæs· virginis partu·
     Clæne acenned· Christus in orbem·
    12 Metod þurh MARIAN· Mundi redemptor·
     & þurh þæne halgan gast· voca frequenter·
²MS.Dominus. Bide helpes hine· Clementem Dominum·²
     Sé onsénded wæs· Summo de throno·
    16 & þære clænan· Clara voce·
     þe gebyrd-boda· bona voluntate·
     ꝥ heo scolde cennan· Christum regem·
     Ealra cyninga cyningc· Casta vivendo·
³ MS. rogo. 20 & þu þa soð-fæstan· Supplex roga·³
     fultumes bidde fricolo· Virginem almam·
⁴ MS. sanctus. & þær æfter tó· omnes sanctos⁴
⁵ MS. justus. Blið-mod bidde· Beatos et justos·⁵
    24 ꝥ hi ealle þe· Unica voce
     þingian to þeodne· Thronum regentem
     Ecum drihtne· Alta polorum
     ꝥ he þine saule· Summus judex
    28 On-fo freolice· factor æternus·
⁶ MS. luce. & he gelæde· in lucem perennem⁶
     þær eadige· Animæ sanctæ·
     Rice restað· Regnis⁷ cælorum·

ORATIO POETICA.

    Then He who rules the world shall have mercy upon thee (N),
    He, the glorious King of the nations, who sitteth upon the throne,
    Ever without end,   Invocation of
                                                            the Father.
4 The friend of the soul.
   May He—the Author of peace—grant thee, in thy life,
   The joys of peace—(He who is) the Health of the world,
   The famous Lord, of great power!
8 And may the faithful Son of the Highest,
   Maker of the universe, receive (thee) into favour,
   Who was, by birth from the noble Virgin,   Invocation of
                                                     the Son.
   Purely brought forth, as Christ, into the world.
12 Lord and Redeemer of the world—by means of Mary,
    And through the Holy Ghost!
    Call upon Him [the Holy Ghost] often,   Invocation of
                                                  the Holy Ghost.
    Pray to Him for help (who is a) merciful Lord,
16 Who was sent-down from the highest throne,
    And (was) to the pure one [Mary] (by His) clear voice
    The messenger of (Christ's) birth, with good will,
    That she should bring forth Christ the King,
20 (She) chaste of life (bring forth) the King of all kings,
    And thou, suppliantly beseech the true one,
    Pray for help fervently to the benign Virgin.   Invocation of
                                                     the Virgin.
    And thereafter moreover all the saints,   Invocation of
                                                     All Saints.
24 Blithe of mood, invoke, the blessed and just ones,
    That they for thee all, with one accord,
    May intercede to the Lord who rules upon the throne,
    (To the) eternal Lord, (who rules) the high places of the skies,
28 That He, the Supreme Judge, thy soul   Final result.
    Will freely receive, (He who is) the Eternal Creator,
    And may He lead (thee) to perennial light,
    Where the blessed sainted souls
32 Rest in the kingdom, the kingdom of heaven!

Paraphrasis Poetica in Orationem Dominicam.

PARAPHRASIS POETICA IN ORATIONEM DOMINICAM.

Pater noster.

Þu éart ure fæder ealles wealdend·
Cyninc on wuldre· forðam we clypiað to þe·
áre biddað nu ðu ýþost miht·
4 sawle alysan þu híg sændest ǽr·
þurh þine æþelan hand into þam flæsce
ac hwar cymð heo nú·
buton þu engla god eft hiʒ alýse·
8 sawle of synnum þurh ðine soðan miht.

Qui es in celis.

Ðu eart on heofonum· hiht and frofor·
Blissa beorhtost· ealle¹ abúgað to þe
þinra gasta þrym· anre stǽfne·
12 clypiað to criste cweþað ealle þus
halig eart þu halig· heofon-engla cyningc·
drihten úre· & þine domas synd
rihte & rume· ræcað ² efne gehwam
16 æʒhwilcum men agen gewyrhta·
wel bið ðam þe wyrcð willan þinne.

Sanctificetur nomen tuum.

Swa is gehalgod þin heah nama·
swiðe mærlice manegum gereordum· ³
20 twa & hund seofontig· þæs þe secgað bec·
ꝥ þu engla god· ealle gesettest·
ælcere þeode· þeaw & wisan·
þa wurþiað þin weorc· wordum and dædum·
24 þurh gecynd clypiað· & crist heriað·
& þin lof lædað lifigenda god·
swa þu eart geæþelod· geond ealle world.

¹ MS. ealla.

² MS. ræcð.

³ MS. geweordum.

POETICAL PARAPHRASE OF THE LORD'S PRAYER.

Pater noster.

   Thou art our father, Ruler of all,   Our Father,
King in Glory, therefore we cry to thee:
For mercy we pray, now thou canst most easily
4 Release our soul, thou before dost send it
Through thy noble hand into the flesh.
But where will it come now,
Unless thou God of Angels again release it:
8 The soul from sins through thy trusty might?

Qui es in celis.

Thou art in heaven, hope and consolation,   Which art in heaven,
Brightest of joys, to thee bow down,
The host of all thy spirits. With one voice
12 They cry to Christ; they all thus exclaim,
Holy art Thou, holy, King of heaven's angels,
Our Lord; and Thy judgments are
Right and ample. They extend yea to each,
16 Each single man, [judgments] for his own works.
Blessed will he be that worketh thy will.

Sanctificetur nomen tuum.

Thy lofty name is so hallowed,   Hallowed be thy name.
Very famously in many tongues
20 Two and seventy, as the books tell
That thou God of angels all arrangedst
Of each people, the manners and customs;
These praise thy work in words and deeds,
24 Through nature they call on and praise Christ
And thy praise they set forth, oh living God,
So thou art honoured through all the world.

Adveniat regnum tuum.

Cum nu & mildsa· mihta waldend·
28 & us þin rice alyf· rihtwis dema
Earda selost & ece lif
¹ MS. lufu.   þar we sib and lufe[1] samod gemetað·
eagena beorhtnys· & ealle mirhðe·
32 þer bið gehyred þin halige lof·
& þin micele miht mannum to frofre·
swa þu engla god eallum blissast·

Fiat voluntas tua.

Gewurðe þin willa· swa þu waldend eart·
36 éce geopenod· geond ealle world·
& þu þe silf eart sodfæst dema·
rice rædbora· geond rumne grund·
swa þin heahsetl is· heah and mære·
40 fæger & wurðlic· swa þin fæder worhte·
æþele & éce· þar ðu on sittest
on þinre swiðran healf· þu eart sunu & fæder
[2] MS. æþela.   ana ægþer· swa is þin æþele[2] gecynd·
44 Micclum gemærsod· & þu monegum helpst·
ealra cyninga þrym· clypast ofer ealle·
bið þin wuldor-word· wide gehyred·
þonne þu þine fyrde fægere geblissast·
48 sylest miht and mund· micclum herige·
and þe þánciað ðusenda fela·
eal engla þrym anre stæfne.

Sicut in celo.

Swa þe on heofonum· heah þrymnesse·
52 æþele & éce á þánciað·
clæne & gecorene· cristes þegnas·
singað & biddað· soðfæstne god·
are & gifnesse· ealre þeode·
56 þonne þu him tiðast týreadig cyningc·

Adveniat regnum tuum.

 Come now and pity, Ruler of might,   Thy kingdom come.
28 And grant us thy kingdom, righteous judge,
 Happiest of homes, and eternal life.
 There we shall find peace and love together,
 Brightness of eyes and all mirth :
32 There will be heard thy holy praise,
 And thy great might, for consolation to men,
 So thou, God of Angels, blessest all.

Fiat voluntas tua.

 Let thy will done, as thou art Sovereign,   Thy will be done
36 Eternally revealed, over all the world,
 And thou thyself art righteous judge,
 Mighty counsellor, over the wide earth :
 So is thy high throne, high and grand
40 Fair and honourable : as thy father wrought
 Noble and eternal, where Thou sittest
 On thy own right hand. Thou art Son and Father,
 Both persons in one ; so is thy noble nature
44 Much magnified ; and thou helpest many,
 Thou, the might of all kings, thou callest above all,
 Thy word of might is heard afar.
 When thou thy host joyously makest happy,
48 Thou givest might and protection to the great army,
 And many thousands thank thee,
 The host of all angels with one voice.

Sicut in celo.

 As in heaven in majesty   As in heaven,
52 The noble and immortal servants of Christ
 Pure and elect ever thank thee :
 They sing and pray to the righteous God
 For mercy and the forgiveness of all people ;
56 Then thou grantest to them, glorious king,

swa þu eadmod eart ealre worlde·
sy þe þanc & lof· þinre mildse
wuldor & willa· þu gewurþod eart·
60 on heófonrice heah casere.

Et in terra.

And on eorðan ealra cyninga·
help & heafod· halig læce·
réðe & riht wis· rum heort hláford·
64 þu geæþelodest þe ealle gesceafta·
& tosyndrodest hig· siððan on manega·
sealdest ælcre gecynd agene wisan
& a þine mildse ofer manna bearn

Panem nostrum cotidianum.

68 Swa mid sibbe sænst urne hlaf
dæghwamlice duguðe þinre·
rihtlice dælest
mete þinum mannum· & him mare gehætst·
72 æfter forðsiðe· þines fæder rice·
ꝥ wæs on fruman· fægere gegearwod·
earda selost & éce lif·
gif we soð & riht symle gelæstað·

Da nobis hodie.

76 Syle us to dæg· drihten þine
mildse· and mihta· and ure mod gebig·
þanc & þeawas on þín gewil·
bewyrc us on heortan· haligne gast
80 fæste on innan· & us fultum sile·
ꝥ we moton wyrcan willan þinne·
& þe betæcan tyr-eadig cyningc·
sawle ure on þines silfes hand·

Et dimitte nobis debita nostra.

84 Forgif ús ure synna ꝥ ús ne scamige eft·
drihten úre þonne þu on dóme sitst·

POETICAL PARAPHRASE ON THE LORD'S PRAYER.

As thou art merciful to all the world.
Let there be to thee thanks and praise for thy goodness,
Thou glory and joy! Thou art praised,
60 In the kingdom of heaven as mighty sovereign.

Et in terra.

And on earth of all kings   So in earth.
The help and head, holy healer,
Stedfast and righteous, large-hearted lord.
64 Thou madest for thyself all creatures very good,
And scatteredst them afterwards abroad,
Thou gavest each race its peculiar habits,
And ever thy mercy [thou gavest] over the children of men.

Panem nostrum cotidianum.

68 So with peace thou sendest our loaf   Our daily bread
To thy people daily,
Thou rightly apportionest
Meat to thy men, and to them promisest more
72 After their departure; the kingdom of thy father,
That was in the beginning fairly prepared,
Happiest of homes, and everlasting life,
If we truth and right always perform.

Da nobis hodie.

76 Grant us to-day, Lord,   Give us to-day.
Thy mercy and power, and incline our heart,
Thought and disposition to thy will.
Establish firmly for us in our heart the Holy Ghost within.
80 And grant us help that we may work thy will.
And that we entrust to thee, glorious king,
Our souls into thine own hand.

Et dimitte nobis debita nostra.

84 Forgive us our sins, that we be not hereafter ashamed, And forgive us our trespasses,
Our Lord, when thou in judgment sittest,

& ealle men up arisað·
þe fram wife· & fram were· wurdan acænned·
88 beoð þa gebrosnodon eft· bán mid þam flǽsce·
ealle ansunde eft geworden·
þar we swutollice siððan on cnawað
eal þ we geworhton on worldrice·

¹ MS. búta.
92 betere· & wyrse· ðar beoð bútu¹ ʒeara·
ne magon we hit na dýrnan forðam þe hit drihten wat·
and þar gewitnesse beoð wuldor micele·
heofon waru· & eorð waru· hel waru þridde
96 þonne beoð egsa· geond ealle world·
þar man us tyhhað on dæg twegen eardas·
drihtenes áre oððe deofles þeowet
swa hwaðer wé geearniað her on life·
100 þa hwile þe ure mihta mæste wæron.

Sicut & nos dimittimus debitoribus nostris.

Ac ðonne us alyseð lifigende god·
sawle ure· swa we her gifað

² MS. agilt.
earmon mannum· þe wið us agiltað·²

Et ne nos inducas in temtationem.

104 And na us þu ne læt· laðe beswícan·
on costunga· cwellan & bearnan·
Sawle ure· þeah we sinna fela·
didon for ure disige· dæges & nihtes
108 idele spræce· & unriht weorc·
þine bodu brǽcon· wé þe biddað nu
ælmihtig god· áre & gifnes·
ne læt swa héanlice þin hand geweorc
112 on énde dæge eal forwurðan·

Sed libera nos a malo.

Ac alys us of yfele· ealle we beþurfon
godes gifnesse· agylt habbað·

POETICAL PARAPHRASE ON THE LORD'S PRAYER.   47

    And all men rise up
    That from woman and from man have been born ;
88 Again the wasted bones with the flesh
    Shall become whole again.
    There we shall clearly know hereafter
    All that we wrought in this world,
92 Better and worse, both at hand;
    And we may not conceal it, because the Lord knows it,
    And there as witnesses will be wondrous many
    People of heaven, people of earth, and thirdly people of hell.
96 Then will be terror through all the world,
    Then some one will assign to us at that day two conditions,
    Either the favour of the Lord, or the service of the devil,
    According as we shall have earned either here in life
100 While our powers were at the best.

    Sicut et nos dimittimus debitoribus nostris.

    And then the living God will deliver for us   *As we forgive them that trespass against us.*
    Our souls, as we here forgive
    To frail men who offend against us.

    Et ne nos inducas in temtationem.

104 And let not evil beguile us   *And lead us not into temptation.*
    In temptation, [and] destroy and burn
    Our souls: though we many sins
    Did through our folly day and night,
108 Idle speech, and wrongful work.
    We brake thy commands. We pray thee now,
    Almighty God, for mercy and forgiveness ;
    Let not so miserably thine handy work
112 At the last day all perish.

    Sed libera nos a malo.

    But deliver us from evil. We all need   *But deliver us from evil.*
    God's forgiveness, we have offended

& swiðe gesingod· we ðe soðfæstan god
116 hæriað· and lofiað· swa þu hælend eart
cynebearn gecydd· cwycum & deadum·
æþele & éce ofer ealle þingc·
þu miht on ánre hand· eaðe befealdan·
120 ealne middan eard swilc is mære cyningc·

Amen.

Sy swa þu silf wilt· soðfæst dema·
wé þe engla god ealle heriað
Swa þu eart gewurðod a on worlda forð.

And sinned much, we thee, the faithful God,
116 Laud and praise.   As thou the Saviour art,
Revealed to quick and dead, as a Royal son,
Noble and eternal, above all things,
Thou in one hand canst easily enfold
120 All the world.   Such is the glorious King.

Amen.

Be it as thou thyself wilt, faithful judge.   Amen.
We all laud thee, God of angels,
As thou art honoured, world without end.

Paraphrasis Poetica in Doxologiam.

PARAPHRASIS POETICA IN DOXOLOGIAM.

Gloria.

Sy þe wuldor & lof· wide geopnod
geond ealle þeoda· þanc & willa
mægen and mildse· & ealles modes lufu·
4 soþfæstra sib· and þines silfes dóm·
world gewlitegod· swa þu wealdan miht
eall eorðan mægen· & uplifte
wind· & wolcna wealdest ealle on riht·

Patri et filio et Spiritui Sancto.

8 Ðu éart frofra fæder· & feorhhyrde·
lifes laððeow· leohtes wealdend·
asundrod fram sinnum· swa þin sunu mære·
þurh clæne gecynd· cyninc ofer ealle·
12 beald gebletsod· boca lareow
heah hige frofer·[1]

Sicuta ert in principio.

Swa wæs on fruman· frea mancynnes·
ealre worlde· wlite & frófer·[2]
16 clæne & cræftig· ðu gecyddest þ·
þa ðu éce god ána geworhtest
þurh halige miht· heofonas & eorðan·
eardas· & uplyft· and ealle þinc
20 þu settest on foldan swiðe fela cynna·
and to syndrodest hig· siððan on manega
þu geworhtest· éce god ealle gesceafta·
on six dagum seofoðan þu gerestest·
24 þa wæs geforðod þin fægere weorc·
& þu sunnan dæg silf halgodest·
& þu mærsodest hine manegum to helpe·

[1] MS. frofre.

[2] MS. frofre.

POETIC PARAPHRASE OF THE DOXOLOGY.

Gloria.

Let there be to thee glory and praise wide spread   <small>Glory be</small>
Over all people, thanks and joy,
Might and mercies, and love of all the soul,
4 Peace of the faithful, and thine own majesty,
The world made beautiful. As thou canst sway
All earth's power and the air above,
Wind and clouds thou swayest all aright.

Patri et Filio et Spiritui Sancto.

8 Thou art Father of consolations and guardian of life,   <small>to the Father, and to the Son,</small>
Life's leader, the swayer of light   <small>and to the Holy Ghost.</small>
Severed from sins, as [is] thy glorious Son
Through pure nature, king over all,
12 Strong, blessed, the inspirer of books,
The high consolation of the soul.

Sicuta ert in principio.

As was in the beginning the lord of mankind   <small>As it was in the beginning,</small>
Of all the world brightness and comfort
16 Pure and wise: Thou revealedst that
When thou, eternal God, alone wroughtest
Through thy holy might, heavens and earth,
Countries and air above and all things.
20 Thou settest on earth very many kindreds,
And severest them afterwards abroad.
Thou formedst, eternal God, all creatures
In six days: on the seventh thou didst rest,
24 Then was complete thy fair work,
And thou thyself hallowedst Sunday,
And madest it glorious for a help to many;

þone heaan dæg healdað & friðiað·
28 ealle þa ðe cunnon· cristene þeawas
haligne heortlufan· & þæs hihstan gebod·
on drihtenes naman· se dæg is gewurðod·

Et nunc et semper.

And nu symle þine soðan weorc
32 & þin micele miht manegum swutelað·
swa þine cræftas híg cyðað wide·
ofer ealle world ece standað·
godes hand geweorc groweð swa þu hete·
36 ealle þe heriað· halige dreamas·
clænre stæfne· & cristene bec
eal middan eard· & we men cweðað·
on grunde her· gode lof & þánc·
40 éce willa & þin agen dom·

Et in secula seculorum.

And on worlda world· wunað & rixað·
cyninc innan wuldre· & his þa gecorenan·
heah þrymnesse· halige gastas·
44 wlitige englas & wuldor gife·
soðe sibbe· sawla þancung·
modes mildse· þar is seo mæste lufu
haligdomes heofonas syndon
48 þurh þine écan word æghwær fulle·
swa synd þine mihta ofer middan eard:
swutole & gesýne þæt þu hig silf worhtest·

Amen.

We ꝥ soðlice secgað ealle
52 þurh clæne gecynd· þu eart cyninc on riht·
clæne & cræftig· þu gecyddest ꝥ·
þa ðu mihtig god man geworhtest·
& him on dydest orð and sawle·
56 sealdest word & gewitt · & wæstma gecynd·
cyddest ðine cræftas· swilc is cristes miht·

That high day all will hold and observe
28 Who understand Christian customs,
Holy love of heart, and the commands of the Highest,
In the Lord's name the day is honoured.

Et nunc et semper.

And now ever thy true works   is now and ever shall be,
32 And thy great might is manifest to many,
As they make known abroad thy wisdom
They stand eternal over all the world,
God's handy work grows as thou didst command,
36 All praise thee, the holy choruses
With pure voice, and Christian books,
All the earth ; and we men say
Here on earth, " Be praise and thanks to God
40 Eternal joy, and thine own majesty."

Et in secula seculorum.

And for ever and ever he dwells and reigns   world without end.
King in glory, his chosen ones
In high majesty, holy spirits,
44 Glorious angels, and mighty powers,
Faithful peace, thankfulness of souls,
Kindness of heart. There is the highest
Love of holiness. The heavens are
48 Through thine eternal word everywhere full :
So is thy might over the earth
Clear and visible as thou thyself wroughtest them.

Amen.

We all say the Amen.   Amen.
52 Through pure nature thou art rightly king,
Pure and wise, thou revealedst that
When thou, mighty God, createdst man,
And into him didst put breath and soul,
56 Gavest him speech and wisdom, and nature of increase,
Thou revealedst to him thy knowledge. Such is Christ's might.

NOTES.

OF DOOMSDAY.

Line 2.—*beþeht*. The better orthography would be *beþeaht*, but it is not unusual for verbs whose stem ends in *ec* to drop the second vowel in the participle. Cf. *gedreccan*, Nic. 6: "þæt he hæfð on slæpe þin wif gedreht." See also March, A.S. Gram. p. 111.

Line 2.—*holte tomiddes*. The same collocation is found in Alfred's Metres, 13, 38. It may be useful to observe such similarity of phraseology, with the object of fixing the date of this poem.

Line 4.—*gehæge*. This word is not given by Bosworth or Grein; the former has the simple form *hege*. The oldest form of the nominative was probably *gehæga*.

Line 5.—*wynwyrta*. Though *wyn* is of common occurrence compounded thus, yet this word seems unique. But *wynburg*, *wynmæg*, and other like compounds, are found in plenty.

Line 6.—*innon*. The unsettled orthography is seen by comparing this form with that in line 1, which is the earlier form. The rime is also to be noticed in the two sections of this line. *Amid the gathering* (*i.e.* of other plants).

Line 8.—*gryre*, properly *horror*; but of the inanimate *wolcn* horror can scarcely be predicated, and therefore the word seems rather to indicate the terrific character or roaring of the wind, and thus almost to be equal to a descriptive adjective.

Line 8.—*gehrered*, perhaps better=agitated, coming from *hreran*, rather than *hreosan*; but see Bosw. 28u. The more usual word is *onhrered*. See Grein, s.v.

Line 11.—*onhefde mid sange*=Germ. *hub an zu singen*. *fers* not given in Grein, and only cited as occurring in a grammar and dictionary by Bosworth.

Line 12.—*gemunde*, an adjective=*gemynde* for *gemyndig*. It occurs in Elene, 1064.

NOTES.

Line 13.—*tid. gemyndgian* is constructed with both accusative and genitive.

Line 15.—*Ic ondræde me eac*, I also feared. The corresponding verb is reflexive in German too.

Line 22.—*þara haligra. haligra* is here the substantive. Cf. Ps. li. 8.

Line 23.—I have written *yfel* rather than *yfeles*, because of the case of *witu*.

Line 25.—*murcnigende*, the word occurs in St. John vii. 33.

Line 27.—*ontynan*, conj. for *ontynen*. This variation is not uncommon. See March, p. 86. Thus we have the classic form *hæbben* in Guthlac (Exon), 644; *habban* in Ps. lxxxv. 16, and *habbon* in Ps. cxxi. 8, each for the present conjunctive.

Line 28.—*hate*, the adverb.

Line 30.—*Breost* must be the acc. plur., as the adjective shows.

Line 30.—*gebedstowe*, one word, though written *divisim* in the MS., cf. Juliana, 376.

Line 32.—*gearnade*, i.e. *ge-earnade*. This past participle is used almost adverbially in the sense of *deservedly*.

Line 34.—*wandian*, like *ontynan*, 27.

Line 42.—*breostes*, etc. These genitives depend on *gylt* understood from the previous clause.

Line 43.—*hæl*, cf. Germ. *heil*=safety.

Line 47.—In altering the MS. in this line, all that has been attempted is to keep as near to the written text as possible while giving a reading which can be construed. It seems most likely that the first *god* had been twice written by some scribe, and that the *i* of *mid* was then altered so as to make an adjective *mod-god* out of the two syllables, after the analogy of *mod-ful*, *mod-þwær*, etc. The Latin text helps but little, being *qui solet allisos sanare*. *Aglidene* is hopelessly corrupt, but as many of the letters of the word as possible have been preserved. It is thus left to the ingenuity of scholars, the exact letters of the MS. being given in the margin.

Line 49.—*nele*, a more usual form is *nelle*; *nyle* also occurs.

Line 49.—*brysan*, not in Grein, and only given by Bosworth on the authority of Somner without a reference.

Line 50.—*gemod*, apparently the same as *mod*, though I have not been able to find an instance of it. But the analogy of *hygd* and *gehygd*, and similar duplicates, is warrant enough for the meaning.

Line 52.—*gedwæscan* is not found elsewhere, but the simple verb *dwæscan* and the compound *todwæscan* occur. The writer of this poem was fond of *ge* as a prefix, v. lines 4, 8.

NOTES. 59

Line 53.—*gesceop*, properly the verb signifies *to shape*, hence *to inform, instruct, warn*. This metaphorical use is not common.

Line 55.—*forstent=forstandeð*. The successive changes seem to have been *forstandð, forstantð, forstent*, the last form also appearing as *forstynt*. The first words of the next line are ſeo soðe hreow.

Line 57.—*sceaða* is written four lines above *scaþa*. Both forms are equally common.

Line 60.—*be-bead*=bade, *i.e.* offered, as in the old expression *bidding of beads* for *offering up prayers*.

Line 61.—*lyt* is used generally followed by a genitive, as *lyt manna* =parum virorum, *lyt freonda*=parum amicorum. Here we have a construction wherein *lyt* seems treated as conjoined with *wordum*, forming a true compound, and therefore having the instrumental case at the end of the whole, after the analogy of such a form as *last-word* =fame after death.

Line 63.—*þa ænlican geatu*, for this construction of the accusative to mark the *way* after *faran*, cf. *For flodwegas*, Riddles (Exon), 37, 9.

Line 68.—*gearugne*. This form, which occurs again in line 91, is not the usual form of the masculine acc. sing., but *gearone*. The original of *gearu* was no doubt *gearug*, cf. *suprà*, 12.

Line 69.—*atihtum*. The weak form *atiht* as the past participle of *ateon* marks a late period of the language, the classic form being *atogen*. The former occurs, however, in Alfred's Boethius, 32, 1, Tit. 32. The tendency has developed in the later language, wherein we have *cleft* and *cloven*; *reft* and *riven*; *lost* and *forlor(e)n*, etc.

Line 73.—*scad*. Not found in this simple form; but as *gescad, gescead*, it is frequent enough. The like phrase to the text occurs in Matt. xii. 36: *Gescead agyldan*.

Line 77.—*horwe*, a very rare word. See the Job in Thwaites Heptateuch, p. 161. It occurs below, line 156.

Line 77.—*afylled*, constructed both with a genitive and (as here) a dative.

Line 79.—*gyte*, a flood: still preserved in the Northern form *goit* or *goyt*, used for the overflow of a milldam, and the channel along which such overflow is conducted.

Line 80.—*beþunga*. The only form in which the nominative is recorded is *beþing*, but the interchange of *i* and *u* in this termination is very common, cf. *wearnung* and *wearning*.

Line 80.—*plaster* is a word of late introduction and rare occurrence.

Line 82.—*greotan*: the usual word in Lowland Scotch for shedding tears still is *to greet*. Here is another riming line.

Line 83.—*þa hwile*, the accusative case used adverbially. The more common form is *þa hwile þe*, followed, as here, by the conjunctive in expressions of indefinite time.

Line 84.—*Nu is halwende*, i.e. *Nu hit is halwende*. The complete expression occurs in Ps. cxviii. 103.

Line 86.—*gnorn þrowast*. The phrase occurs in Beow. 2658.

Line 89.—*men=menn=männ*. Dative singular.

Line 90.—*forhyccan*, i.e. *forhycgan*, the *c* having assimilated the *g* to itself, a very irregular form, for *cc* generally represents a previous *cc*, and *cg=gg* a previous *gi*.

Line 90.—*heaf and wopas*. The combination is common, but the form is more frequently *wop and heaf*.

Line 95.—*heah-þrymme*. Perhaps this ought to be *heah-þrymmes*, but as it stands it is capable of the rendering given to it in the translation.

Line 97.—*forebeacn*. For this plural form compare Grein, Bibl. Ps. cxxxiv. 9.

Line 99.—The alliteration in this line and the next is imperfect, and I am not sure that they should not be written all in one.

Line 101.—*Beorghlið*, as a compound, occurs, see Grein, but the genitive plural *beorga* is much more frequently used of *graves*, and so the sense seems to be, *the doors (hlið=*lid) *of the graves*, rather than the meaning of the compound =*hill slopes*, to which the verbs would not so well apply.

Line 102.—The correction here is not needed. The genitive of *sæ* is sometimes *sǣ* (f.), sometimes *sæs* (m.).

Line 104.—*bið*. This word has been translated here and elsewhere *is*, but in many places *will be*, according as the sense seemed to require. The Saxon having no future was compelled to use this tense for both present and future, and perhaps it may most strictly be termed a sort of aorist. No doubt to this circumstance is due the indefinite character of the modern English present, which may mean an act just in progress, as, *I eat=I am eating*; but in such a sentence as *I eat salt with my potatoes*, has that aorist character which includes past, present, and future all in one. For instances of *bið* used necessarily as a present, see Morris, Blickling Homilies, part i. p. 17. Of him who knows not the brightness of the eternal light, it is said, *se bið blind*. On page 19, speaking of God, the writer says *he bið á wesende* =He is ever living. Yet in the very same sentence *& á biþ ece*, the word may be (as Dr. Morris renders it) translated by our English *shall be*.

NOTES.

Line 105.—*gewuxsað*. If this emendation be correct (and the difference between the þ and the Saxon form of *w* is so slight as to be easily confused), the word is for the more usual form *geweaxeð*.

Line 106.—*dim hiw*. I have not varied the text here, though we probably should read *hiwe* as a dative after the adjective. But the words may be intended to make one compound adjective of the form *bærfot, mildheort, eaðmod*. This being possible, I have allowed them to stand.

Line 107.—Then the stars fall from their stede (or place).

Line 110.—*flecgan*. This is the reading of the MS. The correct orthography would be *flegan* (or *flygan*), a derivative from *fleogan*, as *began* from *beogan*. See Loth, *Etym. Engl. Grammatik*, p. 226.

Line 112.—Literally = *mortem indicantes*, and might = angels of death.

Line 113.—*eored-heapas*. I have not found this compound elsewhere, though similar compounds with *eored* are in use, as *eored-ciest, eored-þreat*, etc.

Line 113.—In the translation I have regarded *upplice* as an adverb, but I think it would be more forcible if taken as the adjective agreeing with *eored-heapas*, and the whole rendered *the legions of heaven*.

Line 114.—*stiþ-mægen*. This compound does not appear elsewhere, but is quite in accordance with other forms from *stið*.

Line 115.—For instances of *ecne* used thus alone as a title of God, see Grein, s.v. *Bihlænan* is the usual form of the verb here.

Line 117.—*sigel-beorht*. *Sigel* being used for the *sun*, and also for a gem or jewel, the compound is capable of a double interpretation. *Gem-bright* is Bosworth's rendering; *sun-bright*, Grein's. The latter seems more in accordance with Scriptural phraseology, cf. Rev. i. 16. The Latin text has *fulget sublimis in alto*.

Line 118.—*weorðian* is not recorded elsewhere as compounded with *be*, the compound form is *geworðian* in other places.

Line 120.—*æghwanum*, a later form, noticed by Bosworth, of the more classic and usual *æghwanon*.

Line 124.—*stent=standeð* (v. *suprâ* 55). The form occurs in Alf. Metr. xx. 171. It has of course, though present, an idea of the future, which is made more vivid by the use of this tense.

Line 124.—*earh*, a later form for *earg*.

Line 125.—*amasod* and *amarod*. I can find no instance of the use of these words or of any verbs from which they may have come. *amarod* seems cognate with *amyrred*, the participle of *amyrran*, to distract, mar.

Line 127.—*surround*, i.e. they will surround. *ymtrymmað* for *ymb-* (or *ymbe-*) *trymmað*.

Line 128.—*aboden*. We should have expected the form to be *abeden*. See March, p. 100.

Line 139.—*þinga*, governed by *eal* in 136.

Line 141.—*ypte oððe cyðde*, for the combination of the two verbs, cf. Bed. iv. 25, and iv. 27.

Line 143.—*alyfed*=concessum, yielded up, set open to every eye.

Line 144.—*Ufenan*, generally means *from above*, and there is not a parallel to the phrase in the text, yet there can be little doubt that *ufenan eall þis* is meant to represent the *insuper* of the Latin. The same words occur again, lines 212 and 221, to represent the same Latin of lines 106 and 138.

Line 145.—*lyft*. As the Lowland Scotch has the same word still for *heaven*, it has been retained in the translation, though not an usual word in English. It seems a pity not to familiarize as much as may be such relics of the old tongue in whatever dialect they may be found, when no attempt is being made to translate into classical English.

Line 146.—*foresteal*. Grein does not give the word, and the orthography in Bosworth is *forstal*, though no instance is given of the occurrence of the word.

Line 147.—*miht*. The more usual form of the instrumental case is *mihte* (see Grein), but *miht* occurs in Cædmon, Exod. ix.: " soðfæst cyning mid his sylfes miht gewyrðode."

Line 147.—For *forwyrnan*, see Bosworth, s.v.

Line 148.—On this line a friend has suggested to me that the reading of the MS. *eah-gemearces*, may be a compound form, after the analogy of *eagþyrl*, *eagdura*, and mean *eye-boundary*, *horizon*. Had this occurred to me, I should not have suggested any other reading, feeling bound, in every case where it is possible, to render the text, rather than correct it. The like change of *g* to *h* has been instanced above, line 124. The Latin text seems to mean *the limitless expanse of air*.

Line 149.—*under roderes ryne*, the expression occurs in Elene, 795.

Line 150.—*emnes*. The usual adverb is *emne*, and the form in the text is found as a noun elsewhere.

Line 152.—*read and reaðe*. The latter of these words is for *reðe*, as it is written in 165. The same collocation in the *Bi Manna Wyrdum* of the Exeter MS., line 46; in Grein's Bibliothek, p. 208, *read reðe gled*.

NOTES. 63

Line 152.—*ræsct*, written *ræscet* (165), from *ræscetan*. See Loth, p. 240.

Line 152.—The more usual form of *efesteð* is *efsteð*.

Line 154.—*brynæ*, i.e. *bryne*.

Line 156.—*afeormad* and *aclænsad*, for the more usual forms in *od*.

Line 158.—*folca unrim*, cf. Germ. *unzahl Leute*.

Line 160.—The adjective *forht* most frequently signifies *timid, terrified*; but in the Hymns in Grein's Bibliothek, x. 56, *on þa forhtan tid*=at that terrible time, and so the adverb in the text may be rendered *terribly* or *fiercely*. The other sense, *in their terror*, would be intelligible, but scarcely seems so apt. The Latin gives no word.

Line 166.—*bærnð* for *beornð*. For an example of this tendency compare also the English *learn* from *leornian*.

Line 167.—*heora heortan . . . syn scyldigra*. For the construction compare Goodwin's Life of St. Guthlac, 22 : *wæs sum his scipes-man þæs foresprecenan Aðelbaldes*. There was one his boatman (viz.) the afore-mentioned Athelbald's.

Line 167.—*horxlice* for *horsclice*. An early example of the tendency which at the present day vulgarizes *ask* into *ax*, though curiously enough the original *acsian* had previously suffered metathesis to come into the modern *ask*.

Line 169.—*æniman* would be better written *divisim, æni man*. The *g* of *ænig* disappeared, but it did not on that account form a compound with the following noun, though here written so.

Line 169.—*arnum*. The adjective *aren*=honourable, meritorious, does not occur elsewhere, but it is regularly formed from *ar*, as *fyren* from *fyr*. The syncopation of the dative plural is like *fyrnum teagum*. Grein, Cr. 733, and Panth. 60, and *gefæstnode fyrnum clommum*, Andreas, 1380. Thus, *be arnum gewyrhtum = meritis* of the Latin text.

Line 170.—*gehende* (prep.) is constructed with a dative case. The earlier expression was *at handum*.

Line 171.—*yrnð* by syncope for *yrneð*.

Line 171.—The construction is *þurh ealle breost-gehyda*. *Breost-gehyda* being the genitive plural governed by *ealle*, which is in the accusative after *þurh*. *Gehyda* for *gehygda*. Grein gives one instance of this orthography from Cædmon, Dan. 732.

Line 173.—*stænt*, written *stent* in line 124, another instance of the fondness of the scribe for the vowel *æ*. Cf. *suprà*, line 154.

Line 173.—*astifad*, cf. *suprà*, line 156.

Line 175.—*hwæt dreogest þu*, cf. Grein, Juliana, line 247.

Line 176.—*gewepan*, only the simple form *wepan* is given in Bosworth and Grein.

Line 177.—Thou servest thyself, *i.e.* thine own pleasure.

Line 178.—*glæd*, adjective used adverbially.

Line 178.—*leofian* is not nearly so common as *libban*.

Line 178.—*galnes* or *galnys*, an unusual word, not in Grein, but given by Bosworth as occurring in the Cottonian copy of Ælfric's glossary.

Line 179.—Perhaps þær is an error for þæm, in which case the sense would be, "thou urgest thyself to that luxury."

Line 179.—*gælsa* is almost as unusual a word as *galnes*. But it occurs below, line 237.

Line 180.—*Forhtas* for *forhtast*. But it has been allowed to stand, because in the later language the second personal pronoun coming after its verb was attached to it, and the last letter of the verb elided, so forhtasþu may be intentional. Cf. Chaucer's frequent *seystow* and *artow*. But it may only be a clerical error, and no indication of the later usage.

Line 180.—*fyrene* for *fyrenne*, masculine accusative singular.

Line 181.—Here we have either a corrupt passage or the construction is most puzzling. *ondræd* is the imperative, and the sentence is =ondræd þu þe sylfum, i.e. dread thou for thyself. The writer seems to have considered the preceding interrogation equal to an imperative sentence, "Wilt thou not fear," equivalent to "Be thou afraid," and then to have followed it up by a direct imperative. For such an indicative (though not interrogative) sentence used for an imperative, cf. Ps. cxviii. 31 : ne wylt þu me gescyndan=do not confound me.

Line 181.—For *ondræd*, cf. Grein, Elene, 81 : Ne ondræd þu þe. But the passage is full of difficulty.

Line 183.—*weana*. It may be that this is to be taken as of the evils done by the tormented, than of the evils done to them. Then the rendering would be, " wages for evil doings." Bosworth quotes Bede (ed. Smith), p. 599, for this sense, which will suit this passage quite as well as that given in the translation.

Line 189.—*susle*, rather *torture, torment*, than with Bosworth's *brimstone*. The line is designed as a description of the *depth* mentioned in the line preceding, which depth existed in hell from of old amid fierce torments.

Line 190.—*synt*. The forms of this plural of the present indicative of the substantive verb are (1) syndon, (2) synd, (3) synt. The second occurs below (217, 285), and in Lár, 19.

Line 191.—*þrece*. This nominative form does not occur. Bosworth gives *þrec*. The genitive plural *gicela* cannot be literally translated.

Line 193.—*ungemetum*. This dative plural used adverbially is of frequent occurrence in the Psalms in Grein's Bibliothek.

Line 195.—*gryrrað*. This verb is not found elsewhere, but there can be no doubt of its meaning from its connexion with *gryre*.

Line 196.—*þis atule gewrixl*. This case pendent (either accusative or nominative) is taken up by the adverb *þærinne*.

Line 200.—*stearc-heard*, probably intended as a compound adjective, cf. *widbrad*.

Line 201.—*na-wiht*, one word; written *naht*, 206.

Line 203.—For similar omissions of the relative, which are not common, cf. Sax. Chr. 963 : *an munac, Brihtnoð wæs gehaten*, a monk (who) was called Brihtnoth. Also Gen. xxix. 29 : *sealde ane þeowene Bala hatte*, i.e. (who) was called Bala.

Line 207.—*unstenc* is not found elsewhere, but as the original signification of *stenc*, and of its derivative verb, was *fragrance, pleasant odour*, *unstenc* is a natural compound to signify the contrary thereof.

Line 208.—*welras*. This word, which is only used in the plural, is elsewhere spelt *weleras*.

Line 214.—*Forhwi* is a literal representation of the *cur* in the Latin text, but the translator does not seem to have known that *cur* might be rendered *because*, otherwise he would have written here *for þy*.

Line 214.—*fyrgende*, evidently intended to translate the present participle *luxurians*, must be from a verb *fyrgan*, of a kindred signification with the verbs *firenian* and *fyrenan*, but such verb does not occur elsewhere.

Line 218.—*sperca*: the orthography elsewhere is *spearca*.

Line 221.—For *wihte* used thus adverbially, see Grein, Cædmon, Dan. 146.

Line 225.—For *þ* we should have expected a repetition of *þær*.

Line 229.—*sauwle*=*sawle* for *sawla*, the usual form of the plural nominative. But *sawle* is found, *Christ and Satan*, 296.

Line 232.—*mid ealle*=Germ. *ganz und gar*. For instances see Alf. Metr. 17, 22; 18, 3; 19, 3.

Line 234.—*hleapað*, i.e. will leap away in flight.

Line 238.—*scyndan*. This, which is the slightest possible alteration of the MS., makes the verb an infinitive, and governed by *gewiteð* (236). But it might be altered and a simpler construction obtained by reading *scyndað*, the plural verb being justified by the expression ælc gælsa. A like construction with the infinitive *slincan* occurs in the next two lines.

Line 242.—*on ende.* Thus used as adverb in Grein, Ps. lviii. 12, lxxviii. 5.

Line 243.—*lað* may either be an adjective, as translated, or a noun =an object of loathing or offence.

Line 251.—*geþeon,* an unusual form of this word. For *þeowan* is very rare. The usual word is *þeowian.*

Line 253.—*þeostra,* i.q. *þeostru.*

Line 253.—*genipð.* This verb does not occur elsewhere, but its meaning is sufficiently evident from its noun.

Line 259.—*gebrasl* is not found, nor *brasl*; but it is for *brastl,* which is the same as the more usual *brastlung.*

Line 261.—*tintrega,* another instance of this masculine nominative is given by Grein from *Christ and Satan,* 497. The more usual word is the neuter *tintreg.*

Line 265.—This line is without alliteration, though containing a rime.

Line 267.—*ricxað,* an intensified form, *riosað* or *rixað* being usual.

Line 275.—*lifað=lyfð.* Third singular present indicative from *leofan.* The more usual verb is *lufian.*

Line 276.—*heah gehrineð.* This emendation seems to most nearly approach the Latin text, *collocat Altithrono. heofon-setle* must be dative, and *hean* could not be taken with it. Bosworth intimates that *gehrinan* is sometimes written *gerinan* (see 28u), but does not give an instance, and the *nn* of the MS. is easily accounted for.

Line 278.—*sylð*; the usual forms are *seleð* and *syleð,* from the latter of which, by a syncopation of which the writer seems very fond, the form in the text is easily reached.

Line 287.—This verse is incomplete, some phrase having fallen out which represented *splendentia castra triumphis.*

Line 290.—*læt* for the more usual *lædeð.* The same part of the verb is spelt *let* in line 294.

Line 290.—Of the last word in this line, *drut,* I can offer no explanation, and have therefore written *brut,* which may have been written as a form of *bryd.* This is however very uncertain. Could *drut* be a contraction for *deorut* ?

Line 291.—*frowe,* evidently the German *frau,* though it is not found elsewhere in Saxon.

Line 299.—*her*=in the world of bliss.

Line 300.—For a similar omission of the relative, cf. 203. þæm must here be singular, as is shown by the verb. *þam* in the next line is plural first, and then singular.

Line 302.—*unbleoh,* a word not found elsewhere, seems to be intended as the equivalent of the *incolumem* of the Latin. The sense may perhaps be arrived at in this way : *bleoh* may, as the name of the colour *blue,* have been applied, as the English word is now, to that which is livid from approaching decay; and thus *unbleoh* would bear the sense of *uncorrupted.* But with a word which only occurs here much must be uncertain.

DE DIE JUDICII.

Page 22.—The Latin text is taken exactly from the edition of Bede as printed in Migne's Bibliotheca Patristica. It is there included among the doubtful works of that Father, and as has been noticed in the Preface, this Latin is also attributed to Alcuin. Either author puts the composition at as early a date as the eighth century.

LÁR.

Page 28.—*Lár*. The title has been adopted from the text of this short poem (line 32). It is evidently intended as a supplement to the Doomsday poem, though no Latin of it is found.

Line 6.—*filige*. This adjective seems to be formed from *ful*, after the manner of *halig* from *hal*, and *sarig* from *sar*. It perhaps would be more correctly written *fulige*. It is left as in the MS., being neither in Grein nor Bosworth.

Line 7.—*oftost symle*. The same collocation occurs in the Juliana of the Cod. Ex., line 20. See Grein, ii. 53.

Line 11.—*adwæscan*, properly used of extinguishing a flame, but this same expression *synne adwæscan* occurs in *Christ and Satan*, 306. See Grein, i. 137.

Line 11.—*fela*, like the Latin *multum*, is followed by a partitive genitive.

Line 16.—*on gemang symle*, nearly equivalent to our *withal*.

Line 23.—If the text be correct, *wylle* is equivalent to *wylle þæt*. I have no instance of such an omission of the accusative before the infinitive in an interrogation. Perhaps we should read *nylle*, and make the sentence declaratory=It will not please.

Line 24.—*mihtu* (i.e. *miht þu*). This coalescing of the pronoun with the verb is a sign of late date. Similar instances are *hafastu* (i.e. *hafast þu*), *Christ and Satan*, 64 (Gr. Bibl. i. p. 131); and *scealtu* (i.e. *scealt þu*), Andreas, 220 (Grein, ii. p. 15).

Line 27.—*forwinnan* seems used in the sense of *oferwinnan*, to overpower, and so eject from a possession. I have not found another instance of the word.

Line 27.—*wealth* as the translation of *welena* implies, of course, every kind of *weal*.

Line 28.—*ealninga*, a late form of the adverb.

Line 29.—*laðum to handa*. The phrase *to handa*, with a similar dative of the person, occurs in Cædmon's Genesis, 1463 : *to handa halgum rince* ; and *to frofre*, with the same construction, as it is in the next line, is found in the same poem, line 955 : *him to frofre*.

Line 32.—*digolice*, literally *secretly*, seems to imply that this precept was some *arcanum*, some deep and efficacious esoteric teaching.

Line 53.—The adverbs are difficult to bring into any English rendering; *earfoðlice* seems to imply the trouble spent in bewailing sin ; *earhlice*, the dread arising from the thought of God's anger.

Line 58.—The sense appears to be, "Find out how thou mayest leave without having received injury from them these talents which have been entrusted to thee."

Line 63.—*hremi*, i.e. *hremig*. This is an instance of the stage through which most of our adjectives in *y* have passed: as *anig* into *any*, *sælig* into *silly*.

Line 66.—*þæt* is certainly pleonastic, and perhaps should be omitted.

ORATIO POETICA.

This prayer, together with the two paraphrases which follow it, have already been printed in Wanley's Catalogue, appended to Hickes's Thesaurus; but as they were evidently a portion of what precedes them in the MS., it has been deemed advisable to reprint them.

Line 1.—*Thænne*. This first word indicates a connexion between what is to come and what has gone before.

Line 1.—*N* (like the *M* or *N* in the Church Catechism) stands as the initial of the name of the person addressed, and this letter may be used as an abbreviation for *Nomen*. It will be seen from the margin of page 36 how very corrupt the Latin portion of this composition is.

In lines 3 and 4 the Latin half of the line has disappeared, and no attempt has been made in reprinting to supply the hiatus, which is merely indicated by the incompleteness of the lines as now arranged. Such other alterations as have been made in the Latin have only been made that the text might be intelligible. The mixture of English and Latin makes the composition of little value grammatically, when in some constructions an English adjective is joined with a Latin noun, the government of the Latin noun being indicated in one way, and that of the adjective in another, as is the case in line 10.

Line 17.—*gebyrd-boda*. A compound not found elsewhere, but regularly formed as *gebyrd-tid*, and *wil-boda*.

Line 21.—*fricolo*. Another ἅπαξ λεγόμενον. Grein, who quotes the word from Wanley, makes it a noun derived *friclan*, to desire, and hence used adverbially it bears the meaning assigned in the translation, "fervently," "eagerly." He also connects it with the adjective *frec*, greedy. A somewhat similar use of an accusative to express the means, though it is not here with a verb, occurs in Cædmon, Gen. 117: Folde wæs þa gyt *græs* ungrene=Not verdant *with grass*; and nearer still in the same poem, line 812, we have unwered *wædo*, unclad in weeds (or clothing), where the instrumental accusative *wædo* is a parallel to *fricolo* in the text.

PARAPHRASE OF THE LORD'S PRAYER.

This text has been published by Grein in his Bibliothek, vol. ii. pp. 287-290, and had been previously produced by Ettmüller, Scôp. 231-234, both having copied it from Wanley. For completing the alliteration in defective lines, and now and then for improving it, Grein has adopted the suggestions of Ettmüller, as where he fills up line 6 with *cyning wuldres*, or, as in line 11, reads *engla* for *gasta* of the text. In the present reprint the text of the MS. has been faithfully represented in most cases in the body of the poem, a transfer of text to the margin having been only made where it was clearly needful to do so.

Line 10.—*ealla*. The alteration by Grein to *ealle* is probably correct (cf. line 12); but as this form *ealla* is found in Alfred's Metres, xx. 128 (Grein ii. 319), it is deemed best to leave it unchanged in this reprint.

Line 15.—*rǽcað*. This is Ettmüller's correction, adopted by Grein, and absolutely necessary.

Line 18.—*heah nama*. Ettmüller would read as one word, but this is not needed.

Line 30.—*sib*. Ettmüller proposes *sibbe*, the more usual form, but these feminines of the strong declension have both forms of the accusative, some words using one form more than the other. Cf. *dǽd*, in which the short form is the more usual. On the other hand, in nouns like *lufu*, the accusative in *e* is so much the more common, that *lufu* of the MS. has been transferred to the margin. This is the only example of *lufu* as accusative which Grein quotes.

Line 33.—*mannum to frofre*, cf. supra *Lár*, line 29.

Line 42.—*þinre*. *sinre* is probably correct, as Grein reads; but it is just possible to attach a meaning to the text of a subtle character, as implying that Son is one with the Father, and for this reason *þinre* is allowed to stand.

Line 43.—The neuter *gecynd* requires us to read *æþele*. The MS. has *þin*, not *þine*, as Wanley prints.

Line 47.—*fægere*, omitted in Wanley, and no suggestion made by Ettmüller or Grein. This reading of the MS. makes the line complete.

Line 55.—*ealre*. Wanley printed *ealra*. Grein suggests *ealre*, which the MS. has.

Line 66.—Grein and Ettmüller read *ælcre gecynde*. The text is very harsh, but may be rendered as an accusative = "But *as to each race* thou gavest [it] its peculiar habits."

Line 68.—*sænst*, i.e. *senst*, which Grein reads; but as the form *sændest* occurs in line 7, it is better to let this peculiarity of the orthography remain.

Line 70.—In this incomplete line Grein adopts Ettmüller's addition of *rumheort hlaford* to fill up. It will do as well as anything else, and occurs in line 63. Probably, therefore, it was not the text in this line.

Line 80.—Here Wanley has omitted *fæste*, which the MS. gives. Ettmüller suggested *frofre*.

Line 82.—Wanley printed *cyninge*. In MS. the last letter is *c*.

Line 86.—So here, too, the MS. has the correct *arisað*, which Wanley gave as *ariseð*.

Line 87.—*acænned*, i.e. *acenned*, but see note on line 68.

Line 88.—*eft*, omitted by Wanley. *gebrosnodon* = *gebrosnodan*.

Line 98.—*are*, thus in MS., Wanley *arc*.

Line 100.—*mihta* MS., Wanley *nihta*. Both these corrections had been made by Grein.

Line 111.—*gifnesse*, as suggested by Grein, though not introduced into his text, is probably correct, but see note on line 30.

Line 118.—*gecydd=gecyðed*. But in a poem so late as this we need not substitute the earlier form, though Grein has done so.

PARAPHRASE OF THE DOXOLOGY.

This poem has also been printed by Grein (vol. ii. pp. 291, 292), and likewise by Bouterwek and Ettmüller from Wanley, see Grein, ii. 411.

Line 13.—*higefrofer=higefrofor*. Grein adds to this line *and halig gast*, which completes the alliteration, but he does not say from whence he derives the addition.

Line 23.—After *dagum* Grein inserts *and on þone*, to make the sense complete, but the words can be understood without the addition.

Line 27.—*heaan=heán*. On this form see March, Ang.-Sax. Gr. page 61, compared with page 59.

Line 27.—*friðiað*. Here Grein adopts the more usual and classic form *freoð-iað*, but this is to give to poem a form which does not belong to it. The other form is found both simply and in composition.

Line 33.—Grein prefers *heo*, referring to *miht* in the previous line, but *hig* can be construed as referring to *weorc*.

Line 47.—Here Grein reads *halige domas*.

Line 49.—Grein shows some inconsistency in adopting *middangeard* as the reading here, but leaving *middaneard* in line 38. MS. and Wanley have *middaneard* in both cases.

INDEX VERBORUM.

The numbers which have no preceding letter refer to the lines of *Doomsday*; those preceded by L to the *Ldr*; those by O to the *Oratio Poetica*; those by P to the *Paraphrase of the Lord's Prayer*; those by D to the *Paraphrase of the Doxology*.

á, L. 65; O. 3; P. 52
abǽred, *part.* 41
aboden, *part.* 128
abugað, P. 10
ac, 276
acende, *præt.* 291
acenned, } *part.* O. 11
acænned, }
aclǽnsad, *part.* 157
acsige, 65
Adames, *gen.* 129
adl, 258
adrifan, L. 46
adwǽscan, L. 11
æddran, *voc. plur.* 26
æfre, 130, 256; L. 71
æfter, O. 22
æghwær, 227; D. 48
æghwilcum, *dat. sing.* P. 16
ægþer, P. 43
æhtum, *d. pl.* L. 34
ælc, *n. sing.* 237
ælce (?), *acc. sing.* P. 66
ælcere, *dat. sing.* P. 22
almes georn, L. 3
ælmessan, *acc. pl.* L. 31
almes-sylen, L. 9
ælmihtig, *nom.* 69; *voc.* P. 111
ælmihtiges, *gen.* 285
ælmihtigne, *acc.* L. 28
æmelnes, } 228
æmelnys, } 260
æmtig, 148
æne (*i.q.* ænne), 128
ænig, 219, 256

ænegum, } *dat. sing.* 187
ænigum, } *dat. sing.* 89, 141, 155
ænigre, *f. s. g.* 202, 224
æniman, 169
ænlican, *acc. pl.* 63; *dat. sg.* 280
ænlicu, *n. f. sing.* 290
ænicum, *dat. sing. masc.* 6
ænne, *acc. sing. masc.* 89
ær, L. 62, 77, 80; P. 4
ærdædum, *d. pl.* 93, 96
ærendracan, *n. pl.* 285
ætes, *g. sing.* L. 44
ætsomne, 142, 164, 171, 190, 234, 274
ættrenum, *dat. sing.* 145
æþelan, *acc. sing. fem.* P. 5
æþele, { *neut. sing. nom.* P. 43
{ *masc. plur.* P. 52
æðelre *fem. gen.* O. 10
afǽred, *part.* 125, 162
afeormad, *part.* 156
afylled, *part.* 77
age, *pres. conj.* 3 *sing.* L. 37
agen, *acc. pl. n.* P. 16
agene, *acc. sing. f.* P. 66
agiltað, P. 104
agiltende (?), 47
agnes, 266
agylt, *part.* P. 115
aht, 204
alǽtan, L. 58
alyf, *imper.* P. 28
alyfed, *part.* 143
alys, *imper.* P. 114
alysan, P. 4; L. 25

74 INDEX VERBORUM.

alyse, *conj. pres.* 2 *sing.* P. 7
alyseð, P. 102
*amarod, *part.* 125
*amasod, *part.* 125
and, 1, 46; L. 7
andrysne, 94
andweard, 273
ane, *acc. f. s.* 163
angryslic, 225
anra, *gen. pl.* 96
anragehwam, *dat. m.* 278
anre, *inst. f. s.* P. 11, 50; *dat. f. s.* 120
ansunde, *nom. pl.* P. 89
ansyn, 202, 224
ansyne, *dat. s.* 120
are, *gen. sing.* P. 3, 55, 111
are, *acc. s.* P. 99
areccan, 186.
arfæstnes, 219, 268
arisað, P. 86
arleas, 174
*arnum, 169
astifad, *part.* 173
astyred, *part.* 114
astyrest, 179
asundrod, *part.* D. 10
atalan, *nom. pl.* 217
atihtum, *dat. pl.* 69
atule, *acc. neut.* 196
aweg, 222
awiht, *adv.* 133
awyrgedum, *dat. pl.* 183

ban, *acc. pl.* 211; *nom. pl.* P. 88
bærnð, 166
be, *prep.* 96, 121
beacnigende, *part.* 112
beald, *adj.* D. 12
bealuwes, *gen. s.* 194
bearn, *acc. pl.* P. 67
bearnan, *i.q.* byrnan, P. 106
bearwe, 1
beatað, 159
beate, 30
bebead, 60
bec, *nom. pl.* D. 37

becwylmað, 203
becumað, 206; L. 52
bedæled, *part.* L. 26
befangen, *part.* L. 26
befealdan, P. 120
beforan, 119, 123
begeat, *præt.* 62
begytan, *inf.* L. 71
behangen, *part.* 289
behlænað, 115
bemurnan, L. 55
bena, *acc. pl.* 60
benum, 33
beo, 7; L. 3
beon, *inf.* 132, 186, 299
beorga, *gen. pl.* 101
beorgan, *inf.* L. 63
beorhtnys, P. 31
beorhtost, P. 10
beortost, 289
beoð, 1 *pers. pl.* 119
beoð, 3 *pl.* 134, 161, 162, 208, 282; P. 88, 92, 95, 97
beseah, *præt.* 241
beswican, P. 105
betæcan, P. 82
betere, P. 92
betweoh, 286
betweox, 296
betwyx, 198, 283, 297
beþeht, *part.* 2
beþunga, 80
beþurfon, P. 114
beweorðod, 118
bewyrc, *imper.* P. 79
biddan, L. 48
biddað, P. 3, 54, 110
bide, *imper.* O. 14
bidde, *pres. ind.* 26, 33, 122
bidde (=bide), *imper.* O. 23; L. 28
bidst, 80
bifað, 99
bitera, 172
biteran, 223
bitere, *acc. f.* 213
biterlice, 166
biterum, 241

INDEX VERBORUM. 75

blawað, 151
blindum, 230, 241
blissa, P. 10
blissast, P. 34
blisse, 224
blissiendum, 284
blissum, L. 63
bliðe, 250, 277; L. 6
bliðmod, O. 23
bliðnesse, 304
blostmum, 289
blowende, *part. pres.* L. 2
boca, D. 12
bodu, P. 10
bræcon, P. 110
braslað, 151
bregað, 112
breged, *part.* 213
breman, 295
breost, 30, 159, 212
breostes, 42
breostgehigdum, 60
breostgehyda, 172
bringað, L. 12
broga, 122
brohte, 119
brucan, 304; L. 61
bryne, 194, 209
brynigum, 211
brysan, 49
brytta, 117, 277
bugað, 101
butan, 200, 203, 205, 207, 304; O. 3
buton, 156
butu, *nom. neut.* P. 92
byrdæn, L. 20
byrgum, 284
byrnað, 230
bysne, 53
byð, 95, 144, 146

care, *acc.* 213
caru, *nom.* 261
casere, *nom.* P. 60
ceald, 192
cealdes, 263
cealdum, L. 47

ceapa, *imper.* L. 34
cennan, O. 18
ceorfað, 168
ceosan, L. 76
clænan, O. 16
clæne, 292; D. 52, 53; P. 53; O. 11
clænre, D. 37
clypast, P. 45
clypiað, P. 2, 12, 24
cnawað, P. 90
cnosl, 129
costunga, P. 106
cræftas, D. 33, 57
crest, 52
criste, 54
cristene, D. 28, 37
cristes, 98
cum, *imper.* P. 27
cumað, 111
cume, 157
cumene, *part.* 120
cunnon, D. 28
cwæð, 25
cweartern, 216
cweman, L. 23
cweðað, D. 38; P. 12
cwelra, 203
cwycum, P. 118
cwyld, 258
cwyldas, 248
cwylmed, *part.* 54, 216
cyddest, D. 57
cyle, 195, 205, 259
cyme, 14, 98·
cymeþ, 71
cymð, 255; P. 6
cynebearn, P. 118
cyningc, P. 56, 80, 121; O. 2
cyric-socnum, L. 47
cyðað, 98; D. 33
cyðde, *præt.* 140
cyþst, 66.

dæda, *acc. pl.* L. 15
dædbote, 85
dædum, 121
dægcuð, 40

INDEX VERBORUM.

dæges, L. 66, 74
dæghwamlice, *adv.* P. 69
dægred, L. 69
dægtide, 135
dælest, P. 70
deadum, P. 118
deað, 112
deaðe, 59
deaðes, 265
dema, *nom.* P. 37, 122
deman, 76, 95, 170
demeð, 71
demst, 87
deofles, P. 99
deoflum, 182
deorc, 106
deriað, L. 42
deriende, *part.* 231
dest, 175
didon, P. 108
digle, 135
digollice, L. 69
digolice, L. 32
dihlan, 20
dihle, 40; L. 51
dim-hiw, 106
dimman, 14
disige, P. 108
dom, 15, 121
domas, P. 14
dome, P. 85
domsetle, 123
dreamas, D. 36
dreccað, 35
dreogest, 175
dreorige, 35
dreosað, 100
dropum, 36
druncen, *acc. s.* L. 74
druncennes, 223; L. 74
*drut, 290
duguðe, P. 69
duna, 99
dwolma, 106
dydest, L. 62
dyrnan, P. 93
dyrne, L. 43

eac, 104, 111, 148, 197, 229
eadegum, 303
eadig, 162
eadige, O. 30
eadignesse, L. 14
eadmod, P. 57; L. 3
eadmolice, L. 48
eagan, 193
eagena, P. 31
eala, 246
eald, 228
eallunc, L. 48
ealne, P. 121
ealninga, *adv.* L. 28
eard, L. 59
earda, P. 29, 74
eardas, D. 19; P. 98
eardes, L. 62
eardian, 302
eardwic, L. 76
earfodlice, L. 54
earh, 124
earhlice, L. 54
earm, 162, 163
earma, 239
earman, 112, 166, 203
earme, 9, 65, 212, 242
earmlice, 187
earmon, P. 104
earmra, 93
earme, 43
earmsceape, 197
earmsceapenra, 23
earmum, 221
earum, 69
eaðe, *adv.* P. 120
ecan, 217, 297
ece, 268, 271, 278
eces, 76; L. 34
ecne, 115, 127
ecnesse, 302
ecum, 37; O. 26
efesteð, *pres.* 152
efne, P. 15
eft, P. 83, 89
ege, *acc.* 164; *nom.* 225; L. 16
egeslic, 94

INDEX VERBORUM. 77

egeslica, 102
egsa, *nom.* P. 97
egsan, *acc.* 180
elles, 201
embe, L. 65
embutan, 114
emnes, 150
ende, 242, 304
endedæge, P. 113
engla, 115, 127, 280
eored-heapas, 113
eorðan, 31, 72, 87
eorðe, 99.
eorðbuendra, 129
eorðwaru, P. 96
eow, 26, 33
eþel, L. 59
eþelrices, L. 73
eþle, L. 62

fæder, 274, 295, 296
fæger, P. 40
fægere, 275; P. 47, 73
færinga, *adv.* 10, 119
færlic, 258
færð, 146
fæste, P. 80; L. 64
fæstenum, L. 45
fæsthafolnes, 236
feddest, L. 80
fedend, *part.* 130
fefur, 258
fehþ, 273
fela, 158, 215; P. 49, 107; L. 11
feonda, L. 64
feondum, L. 26, 30
feor, 236
feorhhyrde, D. 8
feormast, 78
feran, 97
fers, 11
filian, L. 67
filige, L. 6
flæsc, 78, 174, 214
flæsce, P. 5, 88
flæsces, 42, 51
flecgan, 110

fleoh, *imper.* L. 30
fleon, L. 74
flod, 165
flhyð, 222, 239
fo, *conj. pres. 3 sing.* O. 9
folca, 158
foldan, 130; D. 20
forbeacn, 97
forbugan, 154
forbugon, 249
foresteal, 146
forfoh, *imper.* 76
forgif, P. 84
forgifnesse, 68, 01
forhæfdnessum, L. 48
forht, 10
forhtas, 180
forhte, 160
forhyccan, 90
forhwi, 214
forlætan, L. 75, 79
forlæte, L. 29
forleose, L. 18
for-oft, L. 53
forstent, 55
forsworcenum, 198
forswyreð, 108
forð, 304; P. 124
forðam, P. 2, 94; L. 57
forðan, L. 8, 42
forðon, 164
forðsiðe, P. 72
forwurðan, P. 113
forwynned, *part.* L. 27
forwyrnan, 147
frætuað, 275
frea, 19; D. 14
frean, 74, 81, 291
frecnan, 214
fremman, 223; L. 53
freolice, 275; O. 28
freolicum, 296
*fricolo, O. 21
frineð, 300
friðeað, D. 27
frofer, D. 15
frofor, 222; P. 9

INDEX VERBORUM.

frofra, D. 8
frofre, P. 33; L. 26, 30
*frowe, 291
fruman, P. 73
ful, *n.* 205
fule, 188
fultum, 222; P. 80; O. 9
fultumes, O. 21
fyr, 146
fyrde, P. 47
fyre, 165
fyren, 151
fyrcne, 180
fyres, 188
fyrenlustum, 160
fyrgende, 214
fyrhtu, 225
fyste, 29, 160

ga, *imper.* L. 48
gælsa, 237
gælsan, 179
galnysse, 178
gast, P. 79; O. 13
gastum, 183
ge, 27, 34
geæþelod, P. 26
geæþelodest, P. 64
geara, P. 92
gearnade, 32
gearugne, 68, 91
geatu, 63
gebær, *præt.* 131
geban, 128
gebed, 30; L. 8
gebedstowe, 30
gebedum, L. 6
gebeorh, *acc. s.* 223
gebig, P. 77
gebinde, L. 78
gebletsod, D. 12
gebletsodost, 295
geblissast, P. 47
geblysað, 274
gebod, D. 29
gebrasl, 259
gebrosnodon, P. 88

gebyrdboda, O. 17
gecige, 32
geclypede, 137
gecorenan, D. 42
gecorene, P. 53
gecydd, P. 18
gecyddest, D. 16, 53
gecynd, D. 11, 56; P. 24, 43
gecyðe, 45
gedon, L. 60
gedrefed, *part.* 9, 25
gedrefeð, 103
gedwæscan, 52
gedwinað, 231
gedwineð, 233
gedyrsteg, 170
geearniað, P. 100
gefean, 232
gefleman, L. 67
geforðod, D. 24
gefremede, 138, 153
gefremman, 155
gefylde, 208
gefylled, 144, 150
gegearwod, P. 73
gegladað, 220
gehæge, 4
gehælan, 47
gehætst, P. 71
gehalgod, P. 18
gehende, 59, 170
gehrered, 8
gehyda, 172
gehyred, P. 32, 46
gehyreð, 70
gehwæne, L. 64
gehwam, P. 15
gehwilc, 121
gehwylc, 272
gehwylces, 185; L. 23
gehwylcum, 96; L. 37
gelæde, O. 29
gelæstað, P. 75
geleaffullum, 61
gelice, 143
gelicast, 173
geligere, L. 43

INDEX VERBORUM. 79

gelimpeð, 256
gelome, L. 31
gelyfð, L. 33
gemærsod, P. 44
gemang, 280, 282; L. 16
gemearces, 148
gemenged, 190
gemet, 224; L. 50
gemetað, P. 30
gemiltsað, O. 1
gemod, 50
gemonge, 6
gemunde, 12, 21, 24
gemyne, 92
genipð, 253
genipu, 110
geo, *adv.* 182
geond, D. 2; P. 26
geopeniað, 37
geopenod, P. 36
geopnod, D. 1
georne, L. 40
geotan, 82
gereordum, P. 19
gerestest, D. 23
gerinnað, 276
gesælig, 246
gesæligost, 247
gesælða, O. 6
gesceafta, P. 64
gesceop, *pret.* 53
gesecan, L. 72
gesettest, P. 21
gesewen, 202
gesingod, P. 116
gesomnað, L. 41
gestigan, L. 2
gestryndes, L. 22
geswæccan, 206
geswenced, 255
gesweotolude, 134
geswinc, 256
gesworcen, 105
gesylle, L. 21
gesymed, 58
gesyne, D. 50
gesyntum, 248

geteald, 133
geteode, 182
geþancas, 135; L. 52
geþencan, L. 77
geþeode, 282
geþeon, 251
geþohte, 136
geþwærnes, 270
geunne, O. 5
geweald, L. 35
geweorc, D. 35; P. 112
gewepan, 176
gewil, P. 78; L. 39
gewitad, 232
gewiteð, 235, 236
gewitnesse, P. 95
gewitt, D. *acc.* 56
gewlitegod, D. 5
geworden, P. 89
geworhte, 215
geworhtest, D. 17, 22, 54
geworhton, P. 91
gewrixl, 196
gewurðe, P. 35
gewurðod, D. 30; P. 59, 124
gewuxsað, 105
gewyrhta, P. 16
gicela, 191
gif, 86, 300; L. 2, 25, 38, 76
gifað, P. 103
gife, D. 44; L. 49
gifu, 279
gifnes (?), P. 111
gifnesse, P. 55, 115
glæd, 86, 178
glædlice, 272; L. 72
glengað, L. 12
gnagað, 211
gnorn, 86
gnornung, 266
god, 268
goda, 272
gode, 47
godes, 285, 290
godra, L. 12
greotan, 82
grimmum, 189

INDEX VERBORUM.

gristbitung, 226
groweð, D. 35
grunde, 188
gryre, 8, 265
gryrrað, 195
gumena, L. 33
gumene, 122
gyldan, 73
gylta, 39, 56
gyltas, 47, 88, 244; L. 55
gyt, L. 19
gyte, 79

habban, 251
habbað, 164; P. 115
hæfst, 68
hæfð, 163
hæl, 43, 143; L. 49
hæle, 62
hælend, P. 117
hælende, L. 10
hæriað, P. 117
hafa, L. 16
hagulscuras, 264
halgan, O. 13
halgodest, D. 25
halgum, L. 5
haligdomes, D. 47
halige, 283; D. 36, 43; P. 32; L. 8
haligne, D. 29; P. 79
haligra, 22, 281
halwende, 84
handa, L. 29
har, L. 56
hat, *n.* 192
hate, *adj.* 28
heaan, *adj. acc. sing.* D. 27
heaf, 90
heafod, P. 62
heah, D. 43; P. 18
heahfæderas, 283
heah-setl, P. 39
heah-setle, 118
heah-þrymme, 95
healdan, L. 64
healdað, D. 27

healf, P. 42
healic, 279
hean, 276
heanlic, 257
heanlice, P. 112
heanra, 39
heap, 174, 288
heapas, 286
heapum, 281
hearde, 264
heardes, 299
hearmes, 136
hefie, *adj.* L. 56
hefig, L. 20
helle, 189, 192
helme, 2, 118
help, 62; P. 62
helpes, O. 14
helpst, P. 44
hel-waru, P. 96
henða, *acc. pl.* 88
heofena, L. 49
heofenes, 88
heofenlican, 254
heofone, 111
heofon-engla, P. 13
heofonlice, 279
heofonrice, 252
heofonrices, 70
heofonsetle, 276
heofon-waru, P. 96
heonon, L. 46
heonone, 231, 237
heora, 159, 167, 211
heortan, 167
heorte, 136
heortleas, 124
heortlufan, D. 29
heortscræfe, 39
her, *adv.* 84, 156, 299
heriað, D. 36; 24, 123
herige, P. 48
hete, D. 35
hi, L. 56
hider, 111
hig, D. 33; P. 4, 7
higefrofa, D. 13

INDEX VERBORUM.

hiht, P. 9
hihta, 44, 252
higefrofer, D. 13
hilderinc, L. 56
hinder, 240
hlaf, P. 68
hlaford, P. 63
hleahter, 234
hleapað, 234
hleo, 126
hleor, 35
hleorum, 28
hliða, 101
hluttre, L. 8
holte, 2
hopa, 220; L. 9
horwe, 77
horwum, 156
horxlice, 167
hrædra, 75
hremi, L. 63
hreoh, 261
hreosað, 100, 107
hreow, 56
hreowlicum, 75
hryre, 261
hu, 92, 94, 122
hundseofontig, P. 20
hunger, 257
hwære, 140
hwæt, 1, 77, 175, 176, 299
hwan, L. 60
hwaðer, P. 100
hwi, 66, 67, 78, 80, 180, 214
hwile, 88; P. 101
hwilum, 193, 195
hwittra, 288
hwylce, 97
hwyrfð, 288
hy, 210, 282; L. 67
hyge, L. 5
hylt, 274
hym, 215
hyrsta, *gen. pl.* 279

idele, P. 109
ingefor, 63

innan, 1
inne, 38, 197, 204; L. 25
innon, 6
is, 84, 92

la, 65, 175
læce, 46, 66
læçedomes, 81
lædað, P. 25
læne, L. 58
lære, 75; L. 1
læt, 290; P. 105
lage, 163
lange, 66, 143
lar, L. 32
lareow, D. 12
larum, L. 68
latast, 66
lað, 243
laðe, P. 105
laðlic, 205, 262
laðlica, 259
laðlices, 209
laððeow, D. 9
laðum, L. 29
leahtra, 13
leahtrum, 77
leane, 183
lecge, *pres. ind.* 31
lenge, L. 61
leofast, 178
leofest, 243
leoflic, 270
leofne, L. 1
leoht, 218; L. 18, 71
leohtes, 218, 254; L. 34
lichaman, 31
lif, 270; P. 74; L. 66
lifað, 275
life, 243, 299; L. 80
lifes, 81; L. 61
lifigenda, P. 25
lifigende, P. 102
lig, 191, 205
lige, 145, 149
liges, 259
liget, 262

ligspiwelum, 209
ligst, 77
lof, 270; P. 25, 32
lofiaðˇ, P. 117
lufa, L. 4
lufedest, L. 80
lufu, L. 8
lustus, L. 35
lustum, 70
lyft, 145
lyre, 265
lytel, 218
lyt-wordum, 61

mædena, 293
mædenheap, 288
mæg, 46, 147, 169, 186, 249, 299; L. 45
mæge, 110, 223; L. 71
mægen, D. 3
mægðˇa, 158
mæra, O. 7
mæran, 116
mære, 55; P. 121
mærlice, P. 19
mærsodest, D. 26
mærðˇe, 21
mæst, 252
mæste, P. 101
magon, 206; P. 93
man, 84
mán, 37
mandædum, 16
manes, 138
manful, 57
manlican, 131
manna, 103, 185, 195
mannes, 138
mare, P. 71
Maria, 293
mearn, 24
men, 89, 196
meowle, 292
mete, P. 71
metod, 116, 292; O. 7, 12
metodes, L. 16
miccla, L. 9

micel, 55, 92, 122, 128; L. 37
micelnysse, 185
micle, L. 39
miclum, 103, 195
middaneard, D. 38, 49; P. 121
middes, 192
miht, *vb.* 176; L. 67
mihta, P. 27, 101
mihte, 116
mihtig, 19, 12; D. 54
mihtleas, 125
mihtu, L. 24
milde, L. 50
mildsa, P. 27
mildse, D. 3, 45; P. 58, 67, 77
mine, 30
minne, 31
minum, L. 68
mirhðˇe, P. 31
mod, 244; P. 77
modar, 131
mode, 24, 92; L. 6
modum, 284
moldan, 292
mona, 109
morgen, 108
most, L. 61
mot, 251
mote, 301
mund, P. 48
mundbora, L. 52
murcnigende, 26
myltaðˇ, 101

na, P. 93, 105
næfre, 253
næfðˇ, 109
nænig, 186
nænigu, *nom. fem.* 266
nafast, L. 36
naht, 206
naman, D. 30
nan, 146, 200, 222
nane, 147
nanes, 259
nanre, 109
na-wiht, 201

INDEX VERBORUM. 83

ne, 38, 40; P. 84, 93, 105, 112
nearwe, L. 52
nele, 49
neorxnawonges, 64
nerigende, 64
niht, 253; L. 52
nihte, 110
nihtes, P. 108; L. 66, 74
nihtum, 198
nis, 260
nosan, 206
nu, 26; P. 6; L. 1
nuðа, *adv.* 33

ofer, 146; P. 67, 119
oferfylle, L. 75
oferswiðað, 184
ofnes, 194
oft, L. 31
oftost, L. 7
oga, 171
onbindan, 48
ondræd, 181; L. 51
ondræde, 17
ondræt, L. 38
ondydest, D. 55
onfo, O. 28
ongean, L. 66
onginnað, 97
ongyte, L. 55
onhefde, 11
onsended, O. 15
ontynan, 27
on-weg, 237
open, 142
openum, 41
ord, L. 17
ormætnesse, 207
oððe, 67, 94, 97, 131, 132; P. 99; L. 15
owiht, 38

plaster, 80
plega, 234
pices, 199

ræcað, P. 15
ræd, L. 71
rædbora, P. 38
rædwitan, 298
ræplingas, 48
ræscet, 165
ræsct, 152
read, 152
reade, 286
readum, 149
* reaðe, 152
recene, 28, 48, 62
restað, O. 31
reste, L. 13
reðe, 165; P. 63
rican, 74
rice, L. 2, 298
rices, L. 20
ricxað, 267
ricu, 294
riht, 74; D. 52
rihte, P. 15
rigtwis, P. 28, 63
rixað, D. 41
rode, 57
rodera, 298
roderes, 149
rosene, 286
rume, P. 15
rumheort, P. 63
rumne, P. 38
ryne, 149

sæ, 102
sælig, 246
sænst, P. 68
sæt, 1
samod, 126, 250, 267; P. 30
sar, 32, 255
sargunge, 245
sarimod, 226
saule, O. 4, 27; L. 24, 42
sauwle, 42, 299; L. 65, 70
sawle, L. 13
scad, 73
scamige, P. 84

INDEX VERBORUM.

scaþa, 53
scaþelas, L. 58
sceade, 238
sceal, L. 1
scealt, 72, 82, 90 ; L. 54, 58, 63, 72, 87
sceamode, 140
scearplice, 53
sceaðа, 57
scenan, 293
sciman, 254
scinað, 287
scinendan, 293
scolde, O. 18
scræfe, 230
scræfum, 130
scuras, 264
scylda, 140
scyldig, 57, 238
scyldigra, 168
scyndan, 238
scyppend, 73
se, O. 15
sealdest, D. 56 ; P. 66
sealtum, 36
secgan, *inf.* 300
secgað, D. 51 ; P. 20
sefan, 184
selast, 292
selest, 44
selfum, 215
selost, P. 29
seofoðan, D. 23
setle, 276
setlum, 303
settest, D. 20
sib, 220, 267 ; D. 4 ; P. 30
sibbe, 297 ; D. 45 ; P. 68 ; O. 6
sigelbeorht, 117
sigores, 277
sile, P. 80
singað, P. 54
sinnigan, 159
sitst, P. 85
sitt, 117
siðe, L. 72
siððan, P. 65, 90

slæp, 239, 257
slæpes, L. 44
slea, 29
slincan, 240
slitað, 168, 210
sluman, 240
smeage, L. 70
smocan, 51
snawe, 264
sodfæst, P. 37
some, 42
somne, 142, 190
sona, 36, 108
sorge, 190
sorgiendum, 44
sorgum, 244
sorh, 255
soð, 300 ; P. 75
soðan, P. 8
soðe, 56
soðfæst, P. 122
soðfæsta, O. 8
soðfæstan, P. 115 ; O. 20 ; L. 13
soðfæstne, P. 54
soðfæstra, D. 4
spede, 267
spellum, 186
sperca, 218
spræc, 186
spræce, 184 ; P. 109
stæfne, D. 37 ; P. 11, 50
stænt, 173
standað, D. 33
stane, 173
stearc-heard, 200
stedelease, 107
stefne, 200
stent, 124
steorran, 107
sticelum, 179
stiðum, 179
stiþ-mægen, 114
storm, 262
stowa, 188
styllað, 114
styreð, 200
sunnandæg, D. 25

INDEX VERBORUM.

sunne, 108
sunu, 86, 277, 296; P. 42
susle, 152, 189
sweart, 105, 106
sweartum, 198
sweg, 102
swegdon, 3
swegles, 117, 126
swenced, 213
swigast, 67
swige, 220
swincan, L. 75
swiðe, 29; L. 53, 55, 70, 72, 78
swiðlic, 226
swiðlice, 159, 181
swiðor, L. 39
swiðost, L. 42
swiðran, 49; P. 42
swutelað, D. 32
swutole, D. 50
swutollice, P. 90
swylce, 248
swyþe, 49
sy, *conj. pres.* 40, 83, 156; D. 1; P. 58; L. 7
syle, P. 76; L. 31
sylest, P. 48
sylfes, L. 39
sylfne, L. 78
sylfum, 87, 121, 181
syllanne, L. 36
sylð, 278
symle, 287; L. 7, 16; P. 75
synd, 217, 285; L. 19
syndon, D. 47
syndrodest, D. 21
synful, 29
synfullum, 152
synfulra, 18
synlustas, L. 53
synna, 56; L. 55
synne, 79, 229
synnigu, 67
synnum, 78, 87
synscyldigra, 168
synt, 190
syþ, 89

teard, 79
tearas, 82
tearum, 28, 34, 75
teonan, 137
teþ, *acc. pl.* 195
thænne, O. 1
that, 121, 122; L. 2
tid, 83, 176, 214; L. 5
tima, 83
timan, 68, 91
tiðast, P. 56
todæleð, 20
todemeð, 20
tomiddes, 2, 284
torne, 79
tosyndrodest, P. 65
to-wearde, 133
tungan, 42
tunge, 67, 137
tuxlum, 211
twa, P. 20
twegen, P. 98
tyhhað, P. 98
tyreadig, P. 56, 82

þæm, L. 24
þænne, 29, 123; L. 35, 61, 77
þære, 110
þæs, P. 20
þanan, L. 30
þanc, D. 2, 39; P. 58, 78
þanciað, P. 49, 52
þancung, D. 45
þara, 93, 203
þeah, L. 21
þearfe, 176
þearfan, 161
þeawas, D. 28; P. 78
þegnas, P. 53
ðenað, 272
þeoda, D. 2; O. 2
þeod-cyningas, 161
þeode, P. 22
þeodne, 251; O. 25
þeodscipum, 282
þeos, L. 19
þeowast, 177

INDEX VERBORUM.

þeowet, P. 99
þider, 157
ðincaþ, L. 56
þince, L. 50
þincð, 148
þinga, 139
þingc, P. 119
þingian, O. 25
þonne, 71; P. 85; L. 39
þreatum, 281
þrece, 191
þridde, P. 96
þrosma, 191
þrosmes, 199
þrowast, 86
þrym, P. 11, 45, 50
þrymme, 116
þrymnesse, D. 43; P. 51
þunerrad, 263
þurh, 171, 294
þurst, 257
ðusenda, P. 49
þy-læs, L. 35
þynra, L. 70
þystrum, 139
þysse, 232

ufenan, 144, 271
ufenon, 212
ufon, 111
unalyfed, 242
unbleoh, 302
uncræftiga, 239
uncuð, L. 59
uncyst, 237
undædum, 58
under, 149
underfo, 121
ungemet, L. 44
ungerydre, 102
ungemetum, 193
unhyrlican, 11
unrihte, P. 109
unrim, 158
unrot, 10
unrotnes, 227, 260
unstences, 207

unþeawas, L. 41, 79
up, P. 86
upcundra, 303
uplic, 145
uplican, L. 14, 73
uplicum, 46, 297
upplican, L. 76
upplice, 113
uplifte, D. 6
uplyft, D. 19
urne, P. 68
urnon, *pret.* 3

wa, 177
waces, 51
wæccan, L. 4
wædl, 265
wædlan, L. 19
wælgrimme, 210
wæl-hreow, 227
wæron, 132, 133; P. 101
wæstma, D. 56
wæterburnan, 3
wætere, 52
wagedon, 7
waldend, 52; P. 27, 35
wambefylle, L. 40
wandian, 34
wanhydig, 50
wanigendran, 208
wanung, 201
warna, L. 40
wat, P. 94
wealdend, 50; D. 9; P. 1
wealdest, D. 7
weallendes, 199
wean, 199
weana, 183
weard, 70
weardas, 298
wearð, 130
wederum, L. 47
wel, 27, 249, 274
welega, 163
welena, L. 27
welras, 208
wenan, 174

INDEX VERBORUM.　　87

wendað, 197, 244
weorca, L. 12
weorðaþ, 273
weoxon, 5
wepað, 193
wepe, 84
wera, 221
were, P. 87
wereda, 289
werede, 296
werige, 244
werod, 115, 127
werode, 280, 301
wesan, 170
wide, P. 46
wife, P. 87
wiht, 34, 109, 263
wihta, 247
wihte, 202, 221
wile, 89, 95, 154
wille, L. 2, 60
wilnung, L. 44
wilt, P. 122; L. 67, 76
wine, O. 4
winnað, L. 65
winter, 263
wis, L. 4
wisan, P. 22, 66; L. 51
wistum, 233
wite, 92
witegan, 283
witu, 181, 187, 217
witum, 249
wlacan, 51
wlite, D. 15
wlitige, D. 44
wolcn, 8
wolcna, D. 7
woldon, 132
wop, 172, 201
wopas, 90
wope, 35, 45
wopes, 83

wordum, 41, 61; L. 4
worhte, P. 40
worhtest, D. 50
world, D. 5
worldrice, P. 91
worn, 221
wrænnes, 235
wrecan, 89
wrecenda, 154
wudu-beamas, 7
wuldor, 269
wuldorword, P. 46
wuldraþ, 274
wunað, D. 41
wunda, 45
wurdan, P. 87
wurþiað, P. 23
wurðlic, P. 40
wurðmynt, 269
wylle, L. 11
wylspringas, 27
wynwyrta, 5
wyrc, L. 15
wyrcan, P. 81
wyrce, L. 15
wyrcð, P. 17
wyrde, 216
wyrmas, 167, 210
wyrse, P. 92
wyrð, L. 25

yfel, L. 36
yfele, P. 114
yfeles, 174
yld, *nom.* 255
ymbe, L. 70
ymbhwyrft, 72
ymtrymmað, 127
ypte, *præt.* 141
yrnað, 230
yrnð, 171
yrre, 17, 76, 228
yþost, P. 3

Early English Text Society

OFFICERS AND COUNCIL

Honorary Director
PROFESSOR NORMAN DAVIS, M.B.E.
Merton College, Oxford

J. A. W. BENNETT
PROFESSOR BRUCE DICKINS, F.B.A.
A. I. DOYLE
PROFESSOR P. HODGSON
MISS P. M. KEAN
N. R. KER, F.B.A.

C. T. ONIONS, C.B.E., F.B.A.
PROFESSOR J. R. R. TOLKIEN
PROFESSOR D. WHITELOCK, F.B.A.
PROFESSOR R. M. WILSON
PROFESSOR C. L. WRENN

Honorary Secretary
R. W. BURCHFIELD
40 Walton Crescent, Oxford

Bankers
THE NATIONAL PROVINCIAL BANK LTD.
Cornmarket Street, Oxford

THE Subscription to the Society, which constitutes full membership, is £2. 2s. a year for the annual publications, from 1921 onwards, due in advance on the 1st of JANUARY, and should be paid by Cheque, Postal Order, or Money Order crossed 'National Provincial Bank Limited', to the Hon. Secretary, R. W. Burchfield, 40 Walton Crescent, Oxford. Individual members of the Society are allowed, after consultation with the Secretary, to select other volumes of the Society's publications instead of those for the current year. The Society's Texts can also be purchased separately from the Publisher, Oxford University Press, through a bookseller, at the prices put after them in the List, or through the Secretary, by members only, for their own use, at a discount of 2d. in the shilling.

The Early English Text Society was founded in 1864 by Frederick James Furnivall, with the help of Richard Morris, Walter Skeat, and others, to bring the mass of unprinted Early English literature within the reach of students and provide sound texts from which the New English Dictionary could quote. In 1867 an Extra Series was started of texts already printed but not in satisfactory or readily obtainable editions. At a cost of nearly £35,000, 159 volumes were issued in the Original Series and 126 in the Extra Series before 1921. In that year the title *Extra Series* was dropped, and all the publications of 1921 and subsequent years have since been listed and numbered as part of the Original Series. Since 1921 some ninety volumes have been issued. In this prospectus the Original Series and Extra Series for the years 1867–1920 are amalgamated, so as to show all the publications of the Society in a single list. In 1955 the prices of all volumes issued for the years up to 1936 and still available, were increased by one-fifth.

LIST OF PUBLICATIONS
Original Series, 1864–1963. Extra Series, 1867–1920
(One guinea per annum for each series separately up to 1920, two guineas from 1921)

O.S. 1. **Early English Alliterative Poems,** ed. R. Morris. *(Out of print.)* 1864
    2. **Arthur,** ed. F. J. Furnivall. *(Out of print.)* ,,
    3. **Lauder on the Dewtie of Kyngis, &c.,** 1556, ed. F. Hall. *(Out of print.)* ,,
    4. **Sir Gawayne and the Green Knight,** ed. R. Morris. *(Out of print, see O.S. 210.)* ,,
    5. **Hume's Orthographie and Congruitie of the Britan Tongue,** ed. H. B. Wheatley. 5s. 1865
    6. **Lancelot of the Laik,** ed. W. W. Skeat. *(Out of print.)* ,,
    7. **Genesis & Exodus,** ed. R. Morris. *(Out of print.)* ,,
    8. **Morte Arthure,** ed. E. Brock. *(Reprinted 1961.)* 25s. ,,
    9. **Thynne on Speght's ed. of Chaucer,** A.D. 1599, ed. G. Kingsley and F. J. Furnivall. *(Out of print.)* ,,
    10. **Merlin,** Part I, ed. H. B. Wheatley. *(Out of print.)* ,,
    11. **Lyndesay's Monarche, &c.,** ed. J. Small. Part I. *(Out of print.)* ,,
    12. **The Wright's Chaste Wife,** ed. F. J. Furnivall. *(Out of print.)* ,,
    13. **Seinte Marherete,** ed. O. Cockayne. *(Out of print, see O.S. 193.)* 1866
    14. **King Horn, Floriz and Blauncheflur, &c.,** ed. J. R. Lumby, re-ed. G. H. McKnight. *(Reprinted 1962.)* 30s. ,,
    15. **Political, Religious, and Love Poems,** ed. F. J. Furnivall. *(Out of print.)* ,,
    16. **The Book of Quinte Essence,** ed. F. J. Furnivall. *(Out of print.)* ,,
    17. **Parallel Extracts from 45 MSS. of Piers the Plowman,** ed. W. W. Skeat. *(Out of print.)* ,,
    18. **Hali Meidenhad,** ed. O. Cockayne, re-ed. F. J. Furnivall. *(Out of print.)* ,,
    19. **Lyndesay's Monarche, &c.,** ed. J. Small. Part II. *(Out of print.)* ,,
    20. **Richard Rolle de Hampole, English Prose Treatises of,** ed. G. G. Perry. *(Reprinted 1920.)* 7s. ,,
    21. **Merlin,** ed. H. B. Wheatley. Part II. *(Out of print.)* ,,
    22. **Partenay** or **Lusignen,** ed. W. W. Skeat. 7s. 6d. ,,
    23. **Dan Michel's Ayenbite of Inwyt,** ed. R. Morris. *(Out of print.)* ,,
    24. **Hymns to the Virgin and Christ; The Parliament of Devils, &c.,** ed. F. J. Furnivall. *(Out of print.)* 1867
    25. **The Stacions of Rome, the Pilgrims' Sea-voyage, with Clene Maydenhod,** ed. F. J. Furnivall. *(Out of print.)* ,,
    26. **Religious Pieces in Prose and Verse,** from R. Thornton's MS., ed. G. G. Perry. 6s. *(See under 1913.)* ,,
    27. **Levins' Manipulus Vocabulorum,** a rhyming Dictionary, ed. H. B. Wheatley. 14s. ,,
    28. **William's Vision of Piers the Plowman,** ed. W. W. Skeat. A–Text. *(Reprinted 1956.)* 20s. ,,
    29. **Old English Homilies** (1220–30), ed. R. Morris. Series I, Part I. *(Out of print.)* ,,
    30. **Pierce the Ploughmans Crede,** ed. W. W. Skeat. *(Out of print.)* ,,
E.S. 1. **William of Palerne** or **William and the Werwolf,** re-ed. W. W. Skeat. *(Out of print.)* ,,
    2. **Early English Pronunciation,** by A. J. Ellis. Part I. *(Out of print.)* ,,
O.S. 31. **Myrc's Duties of a Parish Priest,** in Verse, ed. E. Peacock. *(Out of print.)* 1868
    32. **Early English Meals and Manners: the Boke of Norture of John Russell, the Bokes of Keruynge, Curtasye, and Demeanor, the Babees Book, Urbanitatis, &c.,** ed. F. J. Furnivall. *(Out of print.)* ,,
    33. **The Book of the Knight of La Tour-Landry,** ed. T. Wright. *(Out of print.)* ,,
    34. **Old English Homilies** (before 1300), ed. R. Morris. Series I, Part II. *(Out of print.)* ,,
    35. **Lyndesay's Works,** Part III: The Historie and Testament of Squyer Meldrum, ed. F. Hall. *(Out of print.)* ,,
E.S. 3. **Caxton's Book of Curtesye,** in Three Versions, ed. F. J. Furnivall. *(Out of print.)* ,,
    4. **Havelok the Dane,** re-ed. W. W. Skeat. *(Out of print.)* ,,
    5. **Chaucer's Boethius,** ed. R. Morris. *(Out of print.)* ,,
    6. **Chevelere Assigne,** re-ed. Lord Aldenham. *(Out of print.)* ,,

The Original and Extra Series of the 'Early English Text Society'

O.S.	36. Merlin, ed. H. B. Wheatley. Part III. On Arthurian Localities, by J. S. Stuart Glennie. (*Out of print.*)	1869
	37. Sir David Lyndesay's Works, Part IV, Ane Satyre of the thrie Estaitis, ed. F. Hall. (*Out of print.*)	,,
	38. William's Vision of Piers the Plowman, ed. W. W Skeat. Part II. Text B. (*Reprinting.*)	,,
	39. The Gest Hystoriale of the Destruction of Troy, ed. D. Donaldson and G. A. Panton. Part I. (*Out of print.*)	,,
E.S.	7. Early English Pronunciation, by A. J. Ellis. Part II. (*Out of print.*)	,,
	8. Queene Elizabethes Achademy, &c., ed. F. J. Furnivall. Essays on early Italian and German Books of Courtesy, by W. M. Rossetti and E. Oswald. (*Out of print.*)	,,
	9. Awdeley's Fraternitye of Vacabondes, Harman's Caveat, &c., ed. E. Viles and F. J. Furnivall. (*Out of print.*)	,,
O.S.	40. English Gilds, their Statutes and Customs, A.D. 1389, ed. Toulmin Smith and Lucy T. Smith, with an Essay on Gilds and Trades-Unions, by L. Brentano. (*Reprinted 1963.*) 55s.	1870
	41. William Lauder's Minor Poems, ed. F. J. Furnivall. (*Out of print.*)	,,
	42. Bernardus De Cura Rei Famuliaris, Early Scottish Prophecies, &c., ed. J. R. Lumby. (*Out of print.*)	,,
	43. Ratis Raving, and other Moral and Religious Pieces, ed. J. R. Lumby. (*Out of print.*)	,,
E.S.	10. Andrew Boorde's Introduction of Knowledge, 1547, Dyetary of Helth, 1542, Barnes in Defence of the Berde, 1542–3, ed. F. J. Furnivall. (*Out of print.*)	,,
	11. Barbour's Bruce, ed. W. W. Skeat. Part I. 14s.	,,
O.S.	44. The Alliterative Romance of Joseph of Arimathie, or The Holy Grail: from the Vernon MS.; with W. de Worde's and Pynson's Lives of Joseph: ed. W. W. Skeat. (*Out of print.*)	1871
	45. King Alfred's West-Saxon Version of Gregory's Pastoral Care, ed., with an English translation, by Henry Sweet. Part I. (*Reprinted 1958.*) 30s.	,,
	46. Legends of the Holy Rood, Symbols of the Passion and Cross Poems, ed. R. Morris. (*Out of print.*)	,,
	47. Sir David Lyndesay's Works, ed. J. A. H. Murray. Part V. (*Out of print.*)	,,
	48. The Times' Whistle, and other Poems, by R. C., 1616; ed. J. M. Cowper. (*Out of print.*)	,,
E.S.	12. England in Henry VIII's Time: a Dialogue between Cardinal Pole and Lupset, by Thom. Starkey Chaplain to Henry VIII, ed. J. M. Cowper. Part II. (*Out of print*, Part I is E.S. 32, 1878.)	,,
	13. A Supplicacyon of the Beggers, by Simon Fish, A.D. 1528–9, ed. F. J. Furnivall, with A Supplication to our Moste Soueraigne Lorde, A Supplication of the Poore Commons, and The Decay of England by the Great Multitude of Sheep, ed. J. M. Cowper. (*Out of print.*)	,,
	14. Early English Pronunciation, by A. J. Ellis. Part III. (*Out of print.*)	,,
O.S.	49. An Old English Miscellany, containing a Bestiary, Kentish Sermons, Proverbs of Alfred, and Religious Poems of the 13th cent., ed. R. Morris. (*Out of print.*)	1872
	50. King Alfred's West-Saxon Version of Gregory's Pastoral Care, ed. H. Sweet. Part II. (*Reprinted 1958.*) 30s.	,,
	51. Þe Liflade of St. Juliana, 2 versions, with translations; ed. O. Cockayne and E. Brock. (*Reprinted 1957.*) 25s.	,,
	52. Palladius on Husbondrie, englisht, ed. Barton Lodge. Part I. 12s.	,,
E.S.	15. Robert Crowley's Thirty-One Epigrams, Voyce of the Last Trumpet, Way to Wealth, &c., ed. J. M. Cowper. (*Out of print.*)	,,
	16. Chaucer's Treatise on the Astrolabe, ed. W. W. Skeat. (*Out of print.*)	,,
	17. The Complaynt of Scotlande, with 4 Tracts, ed. J. A. H. Murray. Part I. (*Out of print.*)	,,
O.S.	53. Old-English Homilies, Series II, and three Hymns to the Virgin and God, 13th-century, with the music to two of them, in old and modern notation, ed. R. Morris. (*Out of print.*)	1873
	54. The Vision of Piers Plowman, ed. W. W. Skeat. Part III. Text C. (*Reprinted 1959.*) 35s.	,,
	55. Generydes, a Romance, ed. W. Aldis Wright. Part I. 3s. 6d.	,,
E.S.	18. The Complaynt of Scotlande, ed. J. A. H. Murray. Part II. (*Out of print.*)	,,
	19. The Myroure of oure Ladye, ed. J. H. Blunt. (*Out of print.*)	,,
O.S.	56. The Gest Hystoriale of the Destruction of Troy, in alliterative verse, ed. D. Donaldson and G. A. Panton. Part II. (*Out of print.*)	1874
	57. Cursor Mundi, in four Texts, ed. R. Morris. Part I, with 2 photolithographic facsimiles. (*Reprinted 1961.*) 25s.	,,
	58. The Blickling Homilies, ed. R. Morris. Part I. (*Out of print.*)	,,
E.S.	20. Lovelich's History of the Holy Grail, ed. F. J. Furnivall. Part I. (*Out of print.*)	,,
	21. Barbour's Bruce, ed. W. W. Skeat. Part II. (*Out of print.*)	,,
	22. Henry Brinklow's Complaynt of Roderyck Mors and The Lamentacyon of a Christen Agaynst the Cytye of London, made by Roderigo Mors, ed. J. M. Cowper. (*Out of print.*)	,,
	23. Early English Pronunciation, by A. J. Ellis. Part IV. (*Out of print.*)	,,
O.S.	59. Cursor Mundi, in four Texts, ed. R. Morris. Part II. (*Out of print.*)	1875
	60. Meditacyuns on the Soper of our Lorde, by Robert of Brunne, ed. J. M. Cowper. 3s.	,,
	61. The Romance and Prophecies of Thomas of Erceldoune, ed. J. A. H. Murray. 12s. 6d.	,,
E.S.	24. Lovelich's History of the Holy Grail, ed. F. J. Furnivall. Part II. (*Out of print.*)	,,
	25. Guy of Warwick, 15th century Version, ed. J. Zupitza. Part I. (*Out of print.*)	,,
O.S.	62. Cursor Mundi, in four Texts, ed. R. Morris. Part III. 18s.	1876
	63. The Blickling Homilies, ed. R. Morris. Part II. (*Out of print.*)	,,
	64. Francis Thynne's Embleames and Epigrams, ed. F. J. Furnivall. 8s. 6d.	,,
	65. Be Domes Dæge (Bede's *De Die Judicii*), &c., ed. J. R. Lumby. (*Out of print.*)	,,
E.S.	26. Guy of Warwick, 15th-century Version, ed. J. Zupitza. Part II. (*Out of print.*)	,,
	27. The English Works of John Fisher, ed. J. E. B. Mayor. Part I. (*Out of print.*)	,,
O.S.	66. Cursor Mundi, in four Texts, ed. R. Morris. Part IV, with 2 autotypes. (*Out of print.*)	1877
	67. Notes on Piers Plowman, by W. W. Skeat. Part I. (*Out of print.*)	,,

The Original and Extra Series of the 'Early English Text Society'

E.S. 28.	Lovelich's Holy Grail, ed. F. J. Furnivall. Part III. (*Out of print.*)	1877
29.	Barbour's Bruce, ed. W. W. Skeat. Part III. 25*s*.	
O.S. 68.	Cursor Mundi, in 4 Texts, ed. R. Morris. Part V. 30*s*.	1878
69.	Adam Davie's 5 Dreams about Edward II, &c., ed. F. J. Furnivall. 6*s*.	"
70.	Generydes, a Romance, ed. W. Aldis Wright. Part II. 5*s*.	"
E.S. 30.	Lovelich's Holy Grail, ed. F. J. Furnivall. Part IV. (*Out of print.*)	"
31.	The Alliterative Romance of Alexander and Dindimus, ed. W. W. Skeat. (*Out of print.*)	"
32.	Starkey's England in Henry VIII's Time. Part I. **Starkey's Life and Letters**, ed. S. J. Herrtage. 9*s*. 6*d*.	"
O.S. 71.	The Lay Folks Mass-Book, four texts, ed. T. F. Simmons. (*Out of print.*)	1879
72.	Palladius on Husbondrie, englisht, ed. S. J. Herrtage. Part II. 6*s*.	"
E.S. 33.	Gesta Romanorum, ed. S. J. Herrtage. (*Reprinted* 1962.) 55*s*.	"
34.	The Charlemagne Romances: 1. **Sir Ferumbras**, from Ashm. MS. 33, ed. S. J. Herrtage. (*Out of print.*)	"
O.S. 73.	The Blickling Homilies, ed. R. Morris. Part III. (*Out of print.*)	1880
74.	English Works of Wyclif, hitherto unprinted, ed. F. D. Matthew. (*Out of print.*)	"
E.S. 35.	Charlemagne Romances: 2. **The Sege off Melayne, Sir Otuell, &c.**, ed. S. J. Herrtage. (*Out of print.*)	"
36.	Charlemagne Romances: 3. **Lyf of Charles the Grete**, ed. S. J. Herrtage. Part I. 19*s*.	"
O.S. 75.	Catholicon Anglicum, an English-Latin Wordbook, from Lord Monson's MS., A.D. 1483, ed., with Introduction and Notes, by S. J. Herrtage and Preface by H. B. Wheatley. (*Out of print.*)	1881
76.	Ælfric's Metrical Lives of Saints, in MS. Cott. Jul. E VII, ed. W. W. Skeat. Part I. (*Out of print.*)	"
E.S. 37.	Charlemagne Romances: 4. **Lyf of Charles the Grete**, ed. S. J. Herrtage. Part II (*Out of print.*)	"
38.	Charlemagne Romances: 5. **The Sowdone of Babylone**, ed. E. Hausknecht. (*Out of print.*)	"
O.S. 77.	Beowulf, the unique MS. autotyped and transliterated, ed. J. Zupitza. (*Re-issued as* No. 245. *See under* 1958.)	1882
78.	The Fifty Earliest English Wills, in the Court of Probate, 1387–1439, ed. F. J. Furnivall. (*Out of print.*)	"
E.S. 39.	Charlemagne Romances: 6. **Rauf Coilyear, Roland, Otuel, &c.**, ed. S. J. Herrtage. 18*s*.	"
40.	Charlemagne Romances: 7. Huon of Burdeux, by Lord Berners, ed. S. L. Lee. Part I. (*Out of print.*)	"
O.S. 79.	King Alfred's Orosius, from Lord Tollemache's 9th-century MS., ed. H. Sweet. Part I. (*Reprinted* 1959.) 30*s*.	1883
79 b.	*Extra Volume.* Facsimile of the Epinal Glossary, ed. H. Sweet. (*Out of print.*)	"
E.S. 41.	Charlemagne Romances: 8. Huon of Burdeux, by Lord Berners, ed. S. L. Lee. Part II. (*Out of print.*)	"
42.	Guy of Warwick: 2 texts (Auchinleck MS. and Caius MS.), ed. J. Zupitza. Part I. (*Out of print.*)	"
O.S. 80.	The Life of St. Katherine, B.M. Royal MS. 17 A. xxvii, &c., and its Latin Original, ed. E. Einenkel. (*Out of print.*)	1884
81.	Piers Plowman: Glossary, &c., ed. W. W. Skeat. Part IV, completing the work (*Out of print.*)	"
E.S. 43.	Charlemagne Romances: 9. Huon of Burdeux, by Lord Berners, ed. S. L. Lee. Part III. (*Out of print.*)	"
44.	Charlemagne Romances: 10. The Foure Sonnes of Aymon, ed. Octavia Richardson. Part I. (*Out of print.*)	"
O.S. 82.	Ælfric's Metrical Lives of Saints, MS. Cott. Jul. E VII, ed. W. W. Skeat. Part II. 20*s*.	1885
83.	The Oldest English Texts, Charters, &c., ed. H. Sweet. (*Reprinted* 1957.) 42*s*.	"
E.S. 45.	Charlemagne Romances: 11. The Foure Sonnes of Aymon, ed. O. Richardson. Part II. (*Out of print.*)	"
46.	Sir Beves of Hamtoun, ed. E. Kölbing. Part I. (*Out of print.*)	"
O.S. 84.	Additional Analogs to 'The Wright's Chaste Wife', O.S. 12, by W. A. Clouston. 1*s*.	1886
85.	The Three Kings of Cologne, ed. C. Horstmann. 20*s*. 6*d*.	"
86.	Prose Lives of Women Saints, ed. C. Horstmann. 14*s*.	"
E.S. 47.	The Wars of Alexander, ed. W. W. Skeat. (*Out of print.*)	"
48.	Sir Beves of Hamtoun, ed. E. Kölbing. Part II. (*Out of print.*)	"
O.S. 87.	The Early South-English Legendary, Laud MS. 108, ed. C. Horstmann. (*Out of print.*)	1887
88.	Hy. Bradshaw's Life of St. Werburghe (Pynson, 1521), ed. C. Horstmann. 12*s*.	"
E.S. 49.	Guy of Warwick, 2 texts (Auchinleck and Caius MSS.), ed. J. Zupitza. Part II. (*Out of print.*)	"
50.	Charlemagne Romances: 12. Huon of Burdeux, by Lord Berners, ed. S. L. Lee. Part IV. (*Out of print.*)	"
51.	Torrent of Portyngale, ed. E. Adam. (*Out of print.*)	"
O.S. 89.	Vices and Virtues, ed. F. Holthausen. Part I. (*Out of print.*)	1888
90.	Anglo-Saxon and Latin Rule of St. Benet, interlinear Glosses, ed. H. Logeman. (*Out of print.*)	"
91.	Two Fifteenth-Century Cookery-Books, ed. T. Austin. (*Out of print.*)	"
E.S. 52.	Bullein's Dialogue against the Feuer Pestilence, 1578, ed. M. and A. H. Bullen. (*Out of print.*)	"
53.	Vicary's Anatomie of the Body of Man, 1548, ed. 1577, ed. F. J. and Percy Furnivall. Part I. (*Out of print.*)	"
54.	The Curial made by maystere Alain Charretier, translated by William Caxton, 1484, ed. F. J. Furnivall and P. Meyer. (*Out of print.*)	"
O.S. 92.	Eadwine's Canterbury Psalter, from the Trin. Cambr. MS., ed. F. Harsley, Part II. (*Out of print.*)	1889
93.	Defensor's Liber Scintillarum, ed. E. Rhodes. 20*s*.	"
E.S. 55.	Barbour's Bruce, ed. W.W. Skeat. Part IV. 6*s*.	"
56.	Early English Pronunciation, by A. J. Ellis. Part V, the present English Dialects. (*Out of print.*)	"
O.S. 94.	Ælfric's Metrical Lives of Saints, MS. Cott. Jul. E VII, ed. W. W. Skeat. Part III. 30*s*.	1890
95.	The Old-English Version of Bede's Ecclesiastical History, re-ed. T. Miller. Part I, 1. (*Reprinted* 1959.) 30*s*.	"
E.S. 57.	Caxton's Eneydos, ed. W. T. Culley and F. J. Furnivall. (*Reprinted* 1962.) 30*s*.	"
58.	Caxton's Blanchardyn and Eglantine, c. 1489, ed. L. Kellner. (*Reprinted* 1962.) 42*s*.	"
O.S. 96.	The Old-English Version of Bede's Ecclesiastical History, re-ed. T. Miller. Part I, 2. (*Reprinted* 1959.) 30*s*.	1891
97.	The Earliest English Prose Psalter, ed. K. D. Buelbring. Part I. (*Out of print.*)	"

4

The Original and Extra Series of the 'Early English Text Society'

E.S.	59. Guy of Warwick, 2 texts (Auchinleck and Caius MSS.), ed. J. Zupitza. Part III. (*Out of print.*)	1891
	60. Lydgate's Temple of Glas, re-ed. J. Schick. (*Out of print.*)	,,
O.S.	98. Minor Poems of the Vernon MS., ed. C. Horstmann. Part I. (*Out of print.*)	1892
	99. Cursor Mundi. Preface, Notes, and Glossary, Part VI, ed. R. Morris. (*Reprinted* 1962.) 25*s*.	,,
E.S.	61. Hoccleve's Minor Poems, I, from the Phillipps and Durham MSS., ed. F. J. Furnivall. (*Out of print.*)	,,
	62. The Chester Plays, re-ed. H. Deimling. Part I. (*Reprinted* 1959.) 25*s*.	,,
O.S.	100. Capgrave's Life of St. Katharine, ed. C. Horstmann, with Forewords by F. J. Furnivall. (*Out of print.*)	1893
	101. Cursor Mundi. Essay on the MSS., their Dialects, &c., by H. Hupe. Part VII. (*Reprinted* 1962.) 25*s*.	,,
E.S.	63. Thomas à Kempis's De Imitatione Christi, ed. J. K. Ingram. (*Out of print.*)	,,
	64. Caxton's Godefroy of Boloyne, or The Siege and Conqueste of Jerusalem, 1481, ed. Mary N. Colvin. (*Out of print.*)	,,
O.S.	102. Lanfranc's Science of Cirurgie, ed. R. von Fleischhacker. Part I. 24*s*.	1894
	103. The Legend of the Cross, &c., ed. A. S. Napier. (*Out of print.*)	,,
E.S.	65. Sir Beves of Hamtoun, ed. E. Kölbing. Part III. (*Out of print.*)	,,
	66. Lydgate's and Burgh's Secrees of Philisoffres ('Governance of Kings and Princes'), ed. R. Steele. (*Out of print.*)	,,
O.S.	104. The Exeter Book (Anglo-Saxon Poems), re-ed. I Gollancz. Part I. (*Reprinted* 1958.) 30*s*.	1895
	105. The Prymer or Lay Folks' Prayer Book, Camb. Univ. MS., ed. H. Littlehales. Part I. (*Out of print.*)	,,
E.S.	67. The Three Kings' Sons, a Romance, ed. F. J. Furnivall. Part I, the Text. (*Out of print.*)	,,
	68. Melusine, the prose Romance, ed. A. K. Donald. Part I, the Text. (*Out of print.*)	,,
O.S.	106. R. Misyn's Fire of Love and Mending of Life (Hampole), ed. R. Harvey. (*Out of print.*)	1896
	107. The English Conquest of Ireland, A.D. 1166–1185, 2 Texts, ed. F. J. Furnivall. Part I. 18*s*.	,,
E.S.	69. Lydgate's Assembly of the Gods, ed. O. L. Triggs. (*Reprinted* 1957.) 25*s*.	,,
	70. The Digby Plays, ed. F. J. Furnivall. (*Out of print.*)	,,
O.S.	108. Child-Marriages and -Divorces, Trothplights, &c. Chester Depositions, 1561–6, ed. F. J. Furnivall. (*Out of print.*)	1897
	109. The Prymer or Lay Folks' Prayer Book, ed. H. Littlehales. Part II. (*Out of print.*)	,,
E.S.	71. The Towneley Plays, ed. G. England and A. W. Pollard. (*Re-issued* 1952.) 30*s*.	,,
	72. Hoccleve's Regement of Princes, and 14 Poems, ed. F. J. Furnivall. (*Out of print.*)	,,
	73. Hoccleve's Minor Poems, II, from the Ashburnham MS., ed. I. Gollancz. (*Out of print.*)	,,
O.S.	110. The Old-English Version of Bede's Ecclesiastical History, ed. T. Miller. Part II, 1. (*Reprinted* 1963.) 30*s*.	1898
	111. The Old-English Version of Bede's Ecclesiastical History, ed. T. Miller. Part II, 2. (*Reprinted* 1963.) 30*s*.	,,
E.S.	74. Secreta Secretorum, 3 prose Englishings, one by Jas. Yonge, 1428, ed. R. Steele. Part I. 24*s*.	,,
	75. Speculum Guidonis de Warwyk, ed. G. L. Morrill. 12*s*.	,,
O.S.	112. Merlin. Part IV. Outlines of the Legend of Merlin, by W. E. Mead. 18*s*.	1899
	113. Queen Elizabeth's Englishings of Boethius, Plutarch, &c., ed. C. Pemberton. (*Out of print.*)	,,
E.S.	76. George Ashby's Poems, &c., ed. Mary Bateson. (*Out of print.*)	,,
	77. Lydgate's DeGuilleville's Pilgrimage of the Life of Man, ed. F. J. Furnivall. Part I. (*Out of print.*)	,,
	78. The Life and Death of Mary Magdalene, by T. Robinson, *c*. 1620, ed. H. O. Sommer. 6*s*.	,,
O.S.	114. Ælfric's Metrical Lives of Saints, ed. W. W. Skeat. Part IV and last. (*Out of print.*)	1900
	115. Jacob's Well, ed. A. Brandeis. Part I. 12*s*.	,,
	116. An Old-English Martyrology, re-ed. G. Herzfeld. 20*s*.	,,
E.S.	79. Caxton's Dialogues, English and French, ed. H. Bradley. 12*s*.	,,
	80. Lydgate's Two Nightingale Poems, ed. O. Glauning. 6*s*.	,,
	81. The English Works of John Gower, ed. G. C. Macaulay. Part I. (*Reprinted* 1957.) 40*s*.	,,
O.S.	117. Minor Poems of the Vernon MS., ed. F. J. Furnivall. Part II. 18*s*.	1901
	118. The Lay Folks' Catechism, ed. T. F. Simmons and H. E. Nolloth. 6*s*.	,,
	119. Robert of Brunne's Handlyng Synne, and its French original, re-ed. F. J. Furnivall. Part I. (*Out of print.*)	,,
E.S.	82. The English Works of John Gower, ed. G. C. Macaulay. Part II. (*Reprinted* 1957.) 40*s*.	,,
	83. Lydgate's DeGuilleville's Pilgrimage of the Life of Man, ed. F. J. Furnivall. Part II. (*Out of print.*)	,,
	84. Lydgate's Reason and Sensuality, ed. E. Sieper. Part I. (*Out of print.*)	,,
O.S.	120. The Rule of St. Benet in Northern Prose and Verse, and Caxton's Summary, ed. E. A. Kock. 18*s*.	1902
	121. The Laud MS. Troy-Book, ed. J. E. Wülfing. Part I. 18*s*.	,,
E.S.	85. Alexander Scott's Poems, 1568, ed. A. K. Donald. (*Out of print.*)	,,
	86. William of Shoreham's Poems, re-ed. M. Konrath. Part I. (*Out of print.*)	,,
	87. Two Coventry Corpus Christi Plays, re-ed. H. Craig. (*See under* 1952.)	,,
O.S.	122. The Laud MS. Troy-Book, ed. by J. E. Wülfing. Part II. 24*s*.	1903
	123. Robert of Brunne's Handlyng Synne, and its French original, re-ed. F. J. Furnivall. Part II. (*Out of print.*)	,,
E.S.	88. Le Morte Arthur, re-ed. J. D. Bruce. (*Reprinted* 1959.) 30*s*.	,,
	89. Lydgate's Reason and Sensuality, ed. E. Sieper. Part II. (*Out of print.*)	,,
	90. English Fragments from Latin Medieval Service-Books, ed. H. Littlehales. (*Out of print.*)	,,
O.S.	124. Twenty-six Political and other Poems from Digby MS. 102, &c., ed. J. Kail. Part I. 12*s*.	1904
	125. Medieval Records of a London City Church, ed. H. Littlehales. Part I. (*Out of print.*)	,,
	126. An Alphabet of Tales, in Northern English, from the Latin, ed. M. M. Banks. Part I. 12*s*.	,,
E.S.	91. The Macro Plays, ed. F. J. Furnivall and A. W. Pollard. (*Out of print.*)	,,
	92. Lydgate's DeGuilleville's Pilgrimage of the Life of Man, ed. Katherine B. Locock. Part III. (*Out of print.*)	,,
	93. Lovelich's Romance of Merlin, from the unique MS., ed. E. A. Kock. Part I. (*Out of print.*)	,,
O.S.	127. An Alphabet of Tales, in Northern English, from the Latin, ed. M. M. Banks. Part II. 12*s*.	1905
	128. Medieval Records of a London City Church, ed. H. Littlehales. Part II. 12*s*.	,,

The Original and Extra Series of the 'Early English Text Society'

O.S. 129.	The English Register of Godstow Nunnery, ed. A. Clark. Part I. 12s.	1905
E.S. 94.	Respublica, a Play on a Social England, ed. L. A. Magnus. (*Out of print. See under* 1946.)	,,
95.	Lovelich's History of the Holy Grail. Part V. The Legend of the Holy Grail, ed. Dorothy Kempe. (*Out of print.*)	,,
96.	Mirk's Festial, ed. T. Erbe. Part I. 14s.	,,
O.S. 130.	The English Register of Godstow Nunnery, ed. A. Clark. Part II. 18s.	1906
131.	The Brut, or The Chronicle of England, ed. F. Brie. Part I. (*Reprinted* 1960.) 25s.	,,
132.	John Metham's Works, ed. H. Craig. 18s.	,,
E.S. 97.	Lydgate's Troy Book, ed. H. Bergen. Part I, Books I and II. (*Out of print.*)	,,
98.	Skelton's Magnyfycence, ed. R. L. Ramsay. (*Reprinted* 1958.) 30s.	,,
99.	The Romance of Emaré, re-ed. Edith Rickert. (*Reprinted* 1958.) 15s.	,,
O.S. 133.	The English Register of Oseney Abbey, by Oxford, ed. A. Clark. Part I. 18s.	1907
134.	The Coventry Leet Book, ed. M. Dormer Harris. Part I. 18s.	,,
E.S. 100.	The Harrowing of Hell, and The Gospel of Nicodemus, re-ed. W. H. Hulme. (*Reprinted* 1961.) 30s.	,,
101.	Songs, Carols, &c., from Richard Hill's Balliol MS., ed. R. Dyboski. (*Out of print.*)	,,
O.S. 135.	The Coventry Leet Book, ed. M. Dormer Harris. Part II. 18s.	1908
135 b.	*Extra Issue.* Prof. Manly's Piers Plowman and its Sequence, urging the fivefold authorship of the Vision. (*Out of print.*)	,,
136.	The Brut, or The Chronicle of England, ed. F. Brie. Part II. (*Out of print.*)	,,
E.S. 102.	Promptorium Parvulorum, the 1st English-Latin Dictionary, ed. A. L. Mayhew. 25s. 6d.	,,
103.	Lydgate's Troy Book, ed. H. Bergen. Part II, Book III. (*Out of print.*)	,,
O.S. 137	Twelfth-Century Homilies in MS. Bodley 343, ed. A. O. Belfour. Part I, the Text. (*Reprinted* 1962.) 25s.	1909
138.	The Coventry Leet Book, ed. M. Dormer Harris. Part III. 18s.	,,
E.S. 104.	The Non-Cycle Mystery Plays, re-ed. O. Waterhouse. (*Out of print.*)	,,
105.	The Tale of Beryn, with the Pardoner and Tapster, ed. F. J. Furnivall and W. G. Stone. (*Out of print.*)	,,
O.S. 139.	John Arderne's Treatises on Fistula in Ano, &c., ed. D'Arcy Power. 18s.	1910
139 b, c, d, e, f,	*Extra Issue.* The Piers Plowman Controversy: b. Dr. Jusserand's 1st Reply to Prof. Manly; c. Prof. Manly's Answer to Dr. Jusserand; d. Dr. Jusserand's 2nd Reply to Prof. Manly; e. Mr. R. W. Chambers's Article; f. Dr. Henry Bradley's Rejoinder to Mr. R. W. Chambers. (*Out of print.*)	,,
140.	Capgrave's Lives of St. Augustine and St. Gilbert of Sempringham, ed. J. Munro. (*Out of print.*)	,,
E.S. 106.	Lydgate's Troy Book, ed. H. Bergen. Part III. (*Out of print.*)	,,
107.	Lydgate's Minor Poems, ed. H. N. MacCracken. Part I. Religious Poems. (*Reprinted* 1961.) 40s.	,,
O.S. 141.	Earth upon Earth, all the known texts, ed., with an Introduction, by Hilda Murray. (*Out of print.*)	1911
142.	The English Register of Godstow Nunnery, ed. A. Clark. Part III. 12s.	,,
143.	The Prose Life of Alexander, Thornton MS., ed. J. S. Westlake. 12s.	,,
E.S. 108.	Lydgate's Siege of Thebes, re-ed. A. Erdmann. Part I, the Text. (*Reprinted* 1960.) 24s.	,,
109.	Partonope, re-ed. A. T. Bödtker. The Texts. (*Out of print.*)	,,
O.S. 144.	The English Register of Oseney Abbey, by Oxford, ed. A. Clark. Part II. 12s.	1912
145.	The Northern Passion, ed. F. A. Foster. Part I, the four parallel texts. 18s.	,,
E.S. 110.	Caxton's Mirrour of the World, with all the woodcuts, ed. O. H. Prior. (*Out of print.*)	,,
111.	Caxton's History of Jason, the Text, Part I, ed. J. Munro. 18s.	,,
O.S. 146.	The Coventry Leet Book, ed. M. Dormer Harris. Introduction, Indexes, &c. Part IV. 12s.	1913
147.	The Northern Passion, ed. F. A. Foster, Introduction, French Text, Variants and Fragments, Glossary. Part II. 18s.	,,
	[An enlarged reprint of O.S. 26, Religious Pieces in Prose and Verse, from the Thornton MS., ed. G. G. Perry. 6s.]	,,
E.S. 112.	Lovelich's Romance of Merlin, ed. E. A. Kock. Part II. (*Reprinted* 1961.) 30s.	,,
113.	Poems by Sir John Salusbury, Robert Chester, and others, from Christ Church MS. 184, &c., ed. Carleton Brown. 18s.	,,
O.S. 148.	A Fifteenth-Century Courtesy Book and Two Franciscan Rules, ed. R. W. Chambers and W. W. Seton. (*Reprinted* 1963.) 25s.	1914
149	Lincoln Diocese Documents, 1450–1544, ed. Andrew Clark. 18s.	,,
150.	The Old-English Rule of Bp. Chrodegang, and the Capitula of Bp. Theodulf, ed. A. S. Napier. 15s.	,,
E.S. 114.	The Gild of St. Mary, Lichfield, ed. F. J. Furnivall. 18s.	,,
115.	The Chester Plays, re-ed. J. Matthews. Part II. (*Reprinted* 1959.) 25s.	,,
O.S. 151.	The Lanterne of Light, ed. Lilian M. Swinburn. (*Out of print.*)	1915
152.	Early English Homilies, from Cott. Vesp. D. XIV, ed. Rubie Warner. Part I, Text. (*Out of print.*)	,,
E.S. 116.	The Pauline Epistles, ed. M. J. Powell. (*Out of print.*)	,,
117.	Bp. Fisher's English Works, ed. R. Bayne. Part II. 18s.	,,
O.S. 153.	Mandeville's Travels, ed. P. Hamelius. Part I, Text. (*Reprinted* 1960.) 25s.	1916
154.	Mandeville's Travels, ed. P. Hamelius. Part II, Notes and Introduction. (*Reprinted* 1961.) 25s.	,,
E.S. 118.	The Earliest Arithmetics in English, ed. R. Steele. 18s.	,,
119.	The Owl and Nightingale, 2 Texts parallel, ed. G. F. H. Sykes and J. H. G. Grattan. (*Reprinted* 1959.) 20s.	,,
O.S. 155.	The Wheatley MS., ed. Mabel Day. 36s.	1917
E.S. 120.	Ludus Coventriae, ed. K. S. Block. (*Reprinted* 1961.) 30s.	,,
O.S. 156.	Reginald Pecock's Donet, from Bodl. MS. 916, ed. Elsie V. Hitchcock. 42s.	1918
E.S. 121.	Lydgate's Fall of Princes, ed. H. Bergen. Part I. (*Out of print.*)	,,

The Original and Extra Series of the 'Early English Text Society'

E.S. 122. Lydgate's Fall of Princes, ed. H. Bergen. Part II. (*Out of print.*)	1918
O.S. 157. Harmony of the Life of Christ, from MS. Pepys 2498, ed. Margery Goates. (*Out of print.*)	1919
158. Meditations on the Life and Passion of Christ, from MS. Add., 11307, ed. Charlotte D'Evelyn. (*Out of print.*)	,,
E.S. 123. Lydgate's Fall of Princes, ed. H. Bergen. Part III. (*Out of print.*)	,,
124. Lydgate's Fall of Princes, ed. H. Bergen. Part IV. (*Out of print.*)	,,
O.S. 159. Vices and Virtues, ed. F. Holthausen. Part II. 14s.	1920
[A re-edition of O.S. 18, Hali Meidenhad, ed. O. Cockayne, with a variant MS., Bodl. 34, hitherto unprinted, ed. F. J. Furnivall. (*Out of print.*)]	,,
E.S. 125. Lydgate's Siege of Thebes, ed. A. Erdmann and E. Ekwall. Part II. (*Out of print.*)	,,
126. Lydgate's Troy Book, ed. H. Bergen. Part IV. 18s.	,,
O.S. 160. The Old English Heptateuch, MS. Cott. Claud. B. IV, ed. S. J. Crawford. (*Out of print.*)	1921
161. Three O.E. Prose Texts, MS. Cott. Vit. A. XV, ed. S. Rypins. (*Out of print.*)	,,
162. Facsimile of MS. Cotton Nero A. x (Pearl, Cleanness, Patience and Sir Gawain), Introduction by I. Gollancz. (*Reprinted* 1955.) 100s.	1922
163. Book of the Foundation of St. Bartholomew's Church in London, ed. N. Moore. (*Out of print.*)	1923
164. Pecock's Folewer to the Donet, ed. Elsie V. Hitchcock. (*Out of print.*)	,,
165. Middleton's Chinon of England, with Leland's Assertio Arturii and Robinson's translation, ed. W. E. Mead. (*Out of print.*)	,,
166. Stanzaic Life of Christ, ed. Frances A. Foster. (*Out of print.*)	1924
167. Trevisa's Dialogus inter Militem et Clericum, Sermon by FitzRalph, and Bygynnyng of the World, ed. A. J. Perry. (*Out of print.*)	,,
168. Caxton's Ordre of Chyualry, ed. A. T. P. Byles. (*Out of print.*)	1925
169. The Southern Passion, ed. Beatrice Brown. (*Out of print.*)	,,
170. Walton's Boethius, ed. M. Science. (*Out of print.*)	,,
171. Pecock's Reule of Cristen Religioun, ed. W. C. Greet. (*Out of print.*)	1926
172. The Seege or Batayle of Troye, ed. M. E. Barnicle. (*Out of print.*)	,,
173. Hawes' Pastime of Pleasure, ed. W. E. Mead. (*Out of print.*)	1927
174. The Life of St. Anne, ed. R. E. Parker. (*Out of print.*)	,,
175. Barclay's Eclogues, ed. Beatrice White. (*Reprinted* 1961.) 35s.	,,
176. Caxton's Prologues and Epilogues, ed. W. J. B. Crotch. (*Reprinted* 1956.) 30s.	,,
177. Byrhtferth's Manual, ed. S. J. Crawford. (*Out of print.*)	1928
178. The Revelations of St. Birgitta, ed. W. P. Cumming. (*Out of print.*)	,,
179. The Castell of Pleasure, ed. R. Cornelius. (*Out of print.*)	,,
180. The Apologye of Syr Thomas More, ed. A. I. Taft. (*Out of print.*)	1929
181. The Dance of Death, ed. F. Warren. (*Out of print.*)	,,
182. Speculum Christiani, ed. G. Holmstedt. (*Out of print.*)	,,
183. The Northern Passion (Supplement), ed. W. Heuser and Frances Foster. (*Out of print.*)	1930
184. The Poems of John Audelay, ed. Ella K. Whiting. (*Out of print.*)	,,
185. Lovelich's Merlin, ed. E. A. Kock. Part III. 30s.	,,
186. Harpsfield's Life of More, ed. Elsie V. Hitchcock and R. W. Chambers. (*Reprinted* 1963.) 45s.	1931
187. Whittinton and Stanbridge's Vulgaria, ed. B. White. (*Out of print.*)	,,
188. The Siege of Jerusalem, ed. E. Kölbing and Mabel Day. 18s.	,,
189. Caxton's Fayttes of Armes and of Chyualrye, ed. A. T. Byles. 25s. 6d.	1932
190. English Mediæval Lapidaries, ed. Joan Evans and Mary Serjeantson. (*Reprinted* 1960.) 20s.	,,
191. The Seven Sages, ed. K. Brunner. (*Out of print.*)	,,
191A.On the Continuity of English Prose, by R. W. Chambers. (*Reprinted* 1957.) 14s.	,,
192. Lydgate's Minor Poems, ed. H. N. MacCracken. Part II, Secular Poems. (*Reprinted* 1961.) 40s.	1933
193. Seinte Marherete, re-ed. Frances Mack. (*Reprinted* 1958.) 30s.	,,
194. The Exeter Book, Part II, ed. W. S. Mackie. (*Reprinted* 1958.) 25s.	,,
195. The Quatrefoil of Love, ed. I. Gollancz and M. Weale. (*Out of print.*)	1934
196. A Short English Metrical Chronicle, ed. E. Zettl. (*Out of print.*)	,,
197. Roper's Life of More, ed. Elsie V. Hitchcock. (*Reprinted* 1958.) 20s.	,,
198. Firumbras and Otuel and Roland, ed. Mary O'Sullivan. (*Out of print.*)	,,
199. Mum and the Sothsegger, ed. Mabel Day and R. Steele. 14s.	,,
200. Speculum Sacerdotale, ed. E. H. Weatherly. (*Out of print.*)	1935
201. Knyghthode and Bataile, ed. R. Dyboski and Z. M. Arend. (*Out of print.*)	,,
202. Palsgrave's Acolastus, ed. P. L. Carver. (*Out of print.*)	,,
203. Amis and Amiloun, ed. MacEdward Leach. (*Reprinted* 1960.) 30s.	,,
204. Valentine and Orson, ed. Arthur Dickson. (*Out of print.*)	1936
205. Tales from the Decameron, ed. H. G. Wright. 20s.	,,
206. Bokenham's Lives of Holy Women (Lives of the Saints), ed. Mary S. Serjeantson. (*Out of print.*)	,,
207. Liber de Diversis Medicinis, ed. Margaret S. Ogden. (*Out of print.*)	,,
208. The Parker Chronicle and Laws (facsimile), ed. R. Flower and A. H. Smith. 84s.	1937
209. Middle English Sermons from MS. Roy. 18 B. xxiii, ed. W. O. Ross. (*Reprinted* 1960.) 42s.	1938
210. Sir Gawain and the Green Knight, ed. I. Gollancz. With Introductory essays by Mabel Day and M. S. Serjeantson. (*Reprinted* 1957.) 10s.	,,
211. Dictes and Sayings of the Philosophers, ed. C. F. Bühler. (*Reprinted* 1961.) 45s.	1939

The Original and Extra Series of the 'Early English Text Society'

212. **The Book of Margery Kempe**, Part I, ed. S. B. Meech and Hope Emily Allen. (*Reprinted* 1961.) 42s. — 1939
213. **Ælfric's De Temporibus Anni**, ed. H. Henel. (*Out of print.*) — 1940
214. **Morley's Translation of Boccaccio's De Claris Mulieribus**, ed. H. G. Wright. (*Out of print.*) — ,,
215. **English Poems of Charles of Orleans**, Part I, ed. R. Steele. (*Out of print.*) — 1941
216. **The Latin Text of the Ancrene Riwle**, ed. Charlotte D'Evelyn. (*Reprinted* 1957.) 31s. 6d. — ,,
217. **Book of Vices and Virtues**, ed. W. Nelson Francis. (*Out of print.*) — 1942
218. **The Cloud of Unknowing and the Book of Privy Counselling**, ed. Phyllis Hodgson. (*Reprinted* 1958.) 40s. — 1943
219. **The French Text of the Ancrene Riwle**, B.M. Cotton MS. Vitellius. F. VII, ed. J. A. Herbert. (*Out of print.*) — ,,
220. **English Poems of Charles of Orleans**, Part II, ed. R. Steele and Mabel Day. (*Out of print.*) — 1944
221. **Sir Degrevant**, ed. L. F. Casson. (*Out of print.*) — ,,
222. **Ro. Ba.'s Life of Syr Thomas More**, ed. Elsie V. Hitchcock and Mgr. P. E. Hallett. (*Reprinted* 1957.) 35s. — 1945
223. **Tretyse of Loue**, ed. J. H. Fisher. (*Out of print.*) — ,,
224. **Athelston**, ed. A. McI. Trounce. (*Reprinted* 1957.) 15s. — 1946
225. **The English Text of the Ancrene Riwle**, B.M. Cotton MS. Nero A. XIV, ed. Mabel Day. (*Reprinted* 1957.) 25s. — ,,
226. **Respublica**, re-ed. W. W. Greg. 18s. 6d. — ,,
227. **Kyng Alisaunder**, ed. G. V. Smithers. Vol. I, Text. (*Reprinted* 1961.) 35s. — 1947
228. **The Metrical Life of St. Robert of Knaresborough**, ed. J. Bazire. (*Out of print.*) — ,,
229. **The English Text of the Ancrene Riwle**, Gonville and Caius College MS. 234/120, ed. R. M. Wilson. With Introduction by N. R. Ker. (*Reprinted* 1957.) 25s. — 1948
230. **The Life of St. George by Alexander Barclay**, ed. W. Nelson. (*Reprinted* 1960.) 28s. — ,,
231. **Deonise Hid Diuinite**, and other treatises related to *The Cloud of Unknowing*, ed. Phyllis Hodgson. (*Reprinted* 1958.) 30s. — 1949
232. **The English Text of the Ancrene Riwle**, B.M. Royal MS. 8 C. 1, ed. A. C. Baugh. (*Reprinted* 1958.) 20s. — ,,
233. **The Bibliotheca Historica of Diodorus Siculus translated by John Skelton**, ed. F. M. Salter and H. L. R. Edwards. Vol. I, Text. 42s. — 1950
234. **Caxton: Paris and Vienne**, ed. MacEdward Leach. 30s. — 1951
235. **The South English Legendary**, Corpus Christi College Cambridge MS. 145 and B.M. M.S. Harley 2277, &c., ed. Charlotte D'Evelyn and Anna J. Mill. Text, Vol. I. 35s. — ,,
236. **The South English Legendary.** Text, Vol. II. 35s. — 1952
[E.S. 87. **Two Coventry Corpus Christi Plays**, re-ed. H. Craig. Second Edition. (*Out of print.*)] — ,,
237. **Kyng Alisaunder**, ed. G. V. Smithers. Vol. II, Introduction, Commentary, and Glossary. 37s. 6d. — 1953
238. **The Phonetic Writings of Robert Robinson**, ed. E. J. Dobson. 28s. — ,,
239. **The Bibliotheca Historica of Diodorus Siculus translated by John Skelton**, ed. F. M. Salter and H. L. R. Edwards. Vol. II. Introduction, Notes, and Glossary. 15s. — 1954
240. **The French Text of the Ancrene Riwle**, Trinity College, Cambridge, MS. R. 14. 7, ed. W. H. Trethewey. 45s. — ,,
241. **Þe Wohunge of ure Lauerd**, and other pieces, ed. W. Meredith Thompson. 32s. — 1955
242. **The Salisbury Psalter**, ed. Celia Sisam and Kenneth Sisam. 84s. — 1955–56
243. **George Cavendish: The Life and Death of Cardinal Wolsey**, ed. Richard S. Sylvester. (*Reprinted* 1961.) 35s. — 1957
244. **The South English Legendary.** Vol. III, Introduction and Glossary, ed. Charlotte D'Evelyn. 25s. — ,,
245. **Beowulf** (facsimile). With Transliteration by J. Zupitza, new collotype plates, and Introduction by N. Davis. 70s. — 1958
246. **The Parlement of the Thre Ages**, ed. M. Y. Offord. 28s. — 1959
247. **Facsimile of MS. Bodley 34** (Katherine Group). With Introduction by N. R. Ker. 42s. — ,,
248. **Þe Liflade ant te Passiun of Seinte Iuliene**, ed. S. R. T. O. d'Ardenne. 30s. — 1960
249. **Ancrene Wisse**, Corpus Christi College, Cambridge, MS. 402, ed. J. R. R. Tolkien. With an Introduction by N. R. Ker. 30s. — ,,
250. **Laȝamon's Brut**, ed. G. L. Brook and R. F. Leslie. Vol. I, Text (first part). 70s. — 1961
251. **Facsimile of the Cotton and Jesus Manuscripts of the Owl and the Nightingale.** With Introduction by N. R. Ker. 42s. — 1962
252. **The English Text of the Ancrene Riwle**, B.M. Cotton MS. Titus D. XVIII, ed. Frances M. Mack, and Lanhydrock Fragment, ed. A. Zettersten. (*At press.*) 35s. — ,,
253. **The Bodley Version of Mandeville's Travels**, ed. M. C. Seymour. (*At press.*) 35s. — 1963
254. **Ywain and Gawain**, ed. Albert B. Friedman and Norman T. Harrington. (*At press.*) 35s. — ,,

The following is a select list of forthcoming volumes. Other texts are under consideration:

Sir Eglamour of Artois, ed. Frances E. Richardson.
Sir Thomas Chaloner: The Praise of Folie, ed. Clarence H. Miller.
Laȝamon's Brut, ed. G. L. Brook and R. F. Leslie, Vols. II and III.
Ælfric: Catholic Homilies, First Series, ed. P. Clemoes.
The Paston Letters, ed. N. Davis.
The English Text of the Ancrene Riwle, edited from all the extant manuscripts:
  Bodleian MS. Vernon, ed. G. V. Smithers.
  B.M. Cotton MS. Cleopatra C. VI, ed. E. J. Dobson.
  Magdalene College, Cambridge, MS. Pepys 2498, ed. A. Zettersten.
The York Plays, re-ed. Arthur Brown.
The Macro Plays, re-ed. Mark Eccles.
The Cely Letters, ed. A. H. Hanham.

April 1963

Publisher
LONDON: THE OXFORD UNIVERSITY PRESS, AMEN HOUSE, E.C. 4

The manufacturer's authorised representative in the EU for product safety is Oxford University Press España S.A. of El Parque Empresarial San Fernando de Henares, Avenida de Castilla, 2 - 28830 Madrid (www.oup.es/en or product.safety@oup.com). OUP España S.A. also acts as importer into Spain of products made by the manufacturer.
Printed and bound by CPI Group (UK) Ltd, Croydon, CR0 4YY

23/03/2026

02076308-0003